Keeping Parrots

Understanding their Care and Breeding

Keeping Parrots

Understanding their Care and Breeding

Alan K. Jones

The Crowood Press

First published in 2011 by
The Crowood Press Ltd
Ramsbury, Marlborough
Wiltshire SN8 2HR

www.crowood.com

British Library Cataloguing-in-Publication Data
A catalogue record for this book is available from the British Library.

ISBN 978 1 84797 263 7

All photographs by Alan K. Jones except where indicated.

This book is dedicated to 'Eric' and all others like him. These birds have enriched my life.

Frontispiece: an outdoor 'parrot picnic' in the Netherlands. (Photo: Jan Hooimeijer)

Typeset by Servis Filmsetting Ltd, Stockport, Cheshire
Printed and bound in India by Replika Press Pvt Ltd

Contents

Foreword

Parrots, parakeets and lovebirds have long had appeal as pets because of their attractive plumage, the relative ease with which they can be tamed and their powers of mimicry. The keeping of such birds and teaching them to talk dates back over 2,000 years, to early civilizations in India and Persia.

When Alexander the Great's army returned from Northern India they brought parrots (probably *Psittacula* parakeets) and from then on, increasingly, the Greeks started to keep such birds. The interest spread to Rome where, later, that great naturalist Pliny the Elder described how best to keep and train the birds. It seems likely that, in addition, the Romans kept African grey parrots, brought back from their expeditions down the Nile.

Between the fifteenth and twentieth centuries parrot-keeping became popular in Europe, especially amongst the aristocracy. In the nineteenth century John Gould, naturalist and artist, took budgerigars from Australia to Great Britain and the popularity of these and other psittacine birds burgeoned.

Over the past decade many books have been published about parrots and their care – in English, in French, in German and in other languages. Is there, one might ask, a need for another? The answer is a resounding 'yes' – for two reasons. Firstly, knowledge and understanding of parrots changes and increases as time goes by; ideas and recommendations propounded even five years ago may no longer be valid or acceptable. Secondly, each author is distinctive: each has his or her own special interests, expertise and style of writing. In this case, for example, Alan Jones is, on his own admission, not an academic researcher – but a practising veterinary surgeon who has been caring for parrots (and other birds) for thirty years. His book reflects this background – practical, down-to-earth and aimed at owners and fellow veterinary practitioners. Notwithstanding, the reader will learn much about the biology and natural history of parrots from the text and from the numerous photographs and diagrams.

In recent years the keeping of so-called 'exotic' animals, including birds, has become increasingly popular and this trend has led to suggestions that the practice should be curtailed, or even banned, on welfare and conservation grounds. To apply such a policy to psittacine birds is unrealistic. Species such as budgerigars, cockatiels and lovebirds have been bred in captivity for decades and, with the selection of birds on the basis of colour and conformation, some can now be considered to be domesticated species. Many other psittacine birds are also being propagated successfully by bird-keepers and zoos and therefore no longer have to be imported from overseas.

Alan Jones has great respect and affection for parrots and this shines through the pages of his book. The science – taxonomy, anatomy, ethology and nutrition – is interspersed with anecdotes about his own and his clients' birds, each of which brings a human touch to the keeping of these fascinating animals. I am in no doubt that parrots, their owners and the veterinary profession all stand to benefit from the publication of this book and I wish them many hours of happy and fruitful reading.

October 2010

John E. Cooper DTVM, FRCPath, FSB, CBiol, FRCVS

Diplomate, European College of Veterinary Pathologists

European Veterinary Specialist, Zoological Medicine (Wildlife Conservation)

University of Cambridge, England: University of Nairobi, Kenya.

Preface

This is not a reference book describing all the thousands of parrots in the world, although many parrots are featured and pictured. There are several books of this type on the market – notably Joseph Forshaw's *Parrots of the World*.

Neither is this a specialist guide to breeding, incubation, and hand-rearing, nor a textbook about parrot diseases – these are also available to the interested reader.

It is rather an overview of parrot-keeping, aimed at both the pet bird owner and the hobbyist keeper. It covers the broad range of parrots available and their suitability for captivity, and then deals with housing, management, feeding, breeding and general care. It is written by a veterinary surgeon who has worked almost exclusively with these birds (and their owners!) for over thirty years, so inevitably there is a scientific slant, yet I have tried not to make it too technical.

The basic information on parrot-keeping the reader may well find in a similar form elsewhere. What I hope I have brought to this volume is firstly an update on current ideas and techniques, but secondly an accumulation of experience acquired over those many years. It is illustrated both by anecdotes about my many patients and by photographs taken mostly by me, or my colleagues and clients.

The ideas and opinions put forward are mine, and are a distillation of my experience with hundreds of parrot-keepers and thousands of their birds. Hopefully this volume will enable people interested in keeping these fascinating birds to better understand their ways, and thereby to avoid some of the many pitfalls that have led to the sort of problems that I have described in this book.

Alan K. Jones BVetMed MRCVS (2011)

CHAPTER 1

Parrots and their Plumage

WHAT IS A PARROT?

If asked to define a parrot, most people would conjure up an image of a squat-bodied, short-tailed bird, with a round head and a large hooked beak. The feather colour could be predominantly green, if they are thinking of an Amazon species or it may be grey with a red tail if they are picturing the popular African grey parrot (*Psittacus erithacus*).

Biggles (Double yellow-headed Amazon (Amazona ochrocephala oratrix) *and Ginger (Blue-fronted Amazon* Amazona aestiva) *– two pet Amazon parrots relaxing at home. (Photo: Lis Perrin)*

Eric, my own African grey parrot (Psittacus erithacus) *on his stand in the garden.*

Peach-faced lovebirds, and a blue variety of the black-masked lovebird (Agapornis spp).

Golden-mantled or yellow rosella variety (Platycercus flaveolus) in an outdoor flight.

However, with over eighty genera including more than 350 species of these birds around the world, the range of size, colour and shape is wide. Body size can range from a tiny 10gm of the Pygmy parrots (*Micropsitta spp* – smaller than a budgerigar) right up to the 1.5kg of the Hyacinthine macaw (*Anodorhynchus hyacinthus*). Body shape ranges from the short and dumpy as described above, and also featured in Poicephalus parrots such as the Meyer's parrot (*Poicephalus meyeri*) and lovebirds, through the more streamlined, long-tailed Asian, African and Australasian parakeets and their South American counterparts the conures, to the heavier bodied but still long-tailed macaws. Along the way is the group that includes the short-bodied, short-tailed birds with very distinctive erectile crest feathers – the cockatoos. But all these birds are parrots.

Oscar, Citron-crested cockatoo (Cacatua sulphurea citrinocristata), showing off his erectile crest feathers, typical of the cockatoos. These feathers may be raised or lowered at will, and indicate excitement, fear, pleasure, distress and other emotions. Note also the large, powerful beak and the short fat tongue typical of most parrots. This sub-species has blue-coloured skin around the eye, and yellow feathering over the ear openings.

Abigail and Faversham, Blue and yellow macaws (Ara ararauna) sharing a stand.

TWO Rs?

The word *parrot* is believed to be derived from the Old French *perroquet*, with two Rs. *Parakeet* supposedly has its root in *periquito*, the Spanish for parrot, or an alternative Old French *paroquet*. Most texts spell 'parrot' with two Rs, and 'parakeet' with just one. Occasional authors use 'parrakeet'. Either way, the spelling of these two words is inconsistent and inexplicable, but in this book I shall follow standard practice and use 'parrot' and 'parakeet'.

The class of vertebrates that includes all birds is Aves, containing several major orders. The order Psittaciformes includes all the parrots, and is in turn sub-divided into three families. Older classifications list these as the Cacatuidae (containing cockatoos and the cockatiel), the Loriidae (lories and lorikeets) and the Psittacidae (all other parrots). More recent DNA studies suggest alternative groupings, and this may well change as further phylogenetic data are amassed. Current thinking separates the Strigopidae as a more primitive family (including just the New Zealand species the Kea, the Kaka and the Kakapo). The Cacatuidae remains as a family as above, while the lories and lorikeets are now absorbed into the Psittacidae as a sub-family Loriinae, being genetically closer to fig parrots and budgerigars.

The group includes species that are critically endangered, through to types that occur in such numbers they are locally considered as pests. Many are popularly kept as pets, or as collections in aviaries, and have been since Roman times, although parrot-keeping reached its peak only in the last century. They are popular because of their colourful plumage, their intelligence and flair for mimicry, their playful behaviour and ability to bond with human beings. The larger species are also long-lived – a two-edged sword that allows for a long-term bonded relationship with a family, but conversely may lead to birds being passed on from home to home as lifestyles change, human relationships break down, or the birds become more

Feral ring-necked parakeet (Psittacula krameri) *fledglings peering from their nest-hole in a tree. This species is now well-established in the wild in many parts of Europe, and will survive harsh winters and compete successfully with native species for food and nest sites.*

troublesome with maturity. This subject will be covered later in the book.

Most species originate from tropical or sub-tropical areas of the world, and are distributed naturally through all continents except Antarctica and Europe. However, many types are also found in temperate grassland regions, and species such as the Quaker or Monk parakeet (*Myiopsitta monachus*) and the Indian ring-necked parakeet (*Psittacula krameri*) have escaped captivity and successfully established feral populations in many parts of Europe and North America. Paradoxically, the only species native to the North American continent became extinct in the early twentieth century because of persecution and habitat destruction. This bird was the Carolina parakeet (*Conuropsis carolinensis*), yet the Ring-neck that has established itself very successfully is a very similar bird in size and shape.

In general, species from the Far East and Australasia show sexual dimorphism (visible differences between male and female), whereas those from Africa and the Americas are mostly sexually monomorphic (male and female indistinguishable – at least to the human eye). This feature will be discussed in more detail later.

Broadly speaking, these birds do not migrate to take advantage of seasonal food sources, climate, or nesting sites, but they are irregularly nomadic, travelling from roosting sites to feeding grounds, and following the various buds, fruits, nuts, and seeds that make up their chosen diet, as these items develop. It follows that parrots of tropical rain forests have less need to travel long distances in search of food compared with those species that live in temperate grassland with wet and dry seasons.

They are social and vocal birds in the wild, often gathering in large family groups, or even larger flocks numbering hundreds of individuals, especially outside of the breeding season. Raucous calls within the group serve to maintain contact and to warn of danger – these are prey species and not predators. The range and variety of these calls is what may initially attract people to keep these birds, but in the long term may also lead to problems with neighbours and progressive lack of tolerance of the volume of screeching.

My grey parrot Eric again, contemplating plastic shapes in a child's toy. Parrots will learn to identify shapes, colours, and textures, with perhaps the most famous and detailed work carried out by Dr Irene Pepperberg with her grey parrot Alex in the USA.

Many parrots are able to mimic sounds including human speech, and this also endears them as human pets. Amazons, budgerigars, macaws and occasionally other species will 'talk', but the undoubted expert is the African grey parrot, which is probably the most popular of the larger species kept as a pet for this very reason. Mynah birds are excellent mimics in terms of their imitating abilities, but grey parrots appear to understand the words they are saying, and use them in the right context. Hence 'hello' and 'goodbye' at appropriate moments, the use of people's names, and activities such as 'bath', 'going shopping' and the like. Parrots are often claimed to have the level of intellect of a three to five-year-old child (with a similar attention span!), and will learn simple tasks and behaviour patterns, and will recognize colours, shapes, textures and numbers (*see* page 60).

ABOVE: *Mingo, ten-day-old Citron-crested cockatoo chick. This cockatoo chick has a fine feathery down and a wide lower mandible to take in food from its parent (or in this case, its human rearer). Note the crop full of food in the lower neck – this sac is a distension of the oesophagus (gullet) that stores and adds enzymes to the food before it passes on down to the stomach. With no feathering present, it is easy to see how large the eyes are in proportion to the skull (although the eyelids are closed at this age – they will start to open at three to four weeks). The tiny ear opening is visible below the right eye.*

DISTINGUISHING FEATURES

Parrots are readily separated from other bird groups by a number of unique features. They have a large hooked upper beak (rostrum) with an undershot lower beak (mandible) with the potential for formidable cracking power yet amazing sensitivity for delicate preening and peeling fruits. There is a very flexible attachment relative to each part of the beak and to the skull. The interior of the open mouth (the gape), however, is nowhere near the width of the flesh-tearing hooked bills of birds of prey (raptors).

BELOW: *Hyacinthine macaw (*Anodorhynchus hyacinthus*), the largest macaw, demonstrating the large hooked beak typical of most parrots. This is a juvenile bird at a breeding project in Brazil. (Photo: Steve Brookes)*

Parrots lay white eggs in nests, holes in trees, or tunnels. Parrot chicks are altricial – hatched with eyes closed and no feathers, totally dependent on their parents for warmth, protection, and food. Birds such as ducks and geese, in contrast, have precocial chicks, which have downy feathers, eyes open, and can run around and swim as soon as they are dry.

Their toes are zygodactyl, with two facing forward and two back. The outer toes I and IV turn backwards (caudally) while the middle toes II and III face forwards. This feature, which is illustrated in a number of pictures throughout

Feet of Bobby, an African grey parrot, showing the zygodactyl toes typical of parrots – two face forwards and two face back.

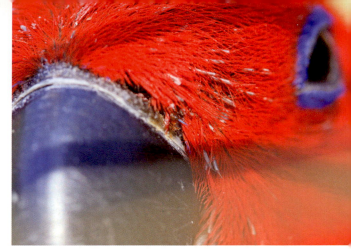

A hen Eclectus parrot, showing the narrow band of skin known as the cere between the beak and the feathers of the head. This fleshy area contains the nostrils: in this bird there is a crusty accumulation around the left nostril, indicative of a nasal discharge.

the book, aids climbing and dexterity – witness parrots holding toys or food items in their feet. Woodpeckers are one of the few other birds that share this trait – most other species have three toes pointing forward and just one backward.

There is an area of naked skin containing the nostrils situated above the upper beak and the forehead known as the cere. It varies in size between species, being virtually non-existent in Eclectus parrots; intermediate in macaws, African

The American bald eagle (Haliaeetus leucocephalus) *showing a much wider gape than the average parrot. Behind the tongue the slit opening into the top of the trachea (windpipe) is visible.*

greys and Amazons; and very prominent in the budgerigar (*Melopsittacus undulatus*). This is coloured differently in adult budgerigars according to their sex, making them visibly sexually dimorphic.

Features that parrots share with other birds but which are not found in other animal groups include pneumatized bones. Most of the long bones and parts of the pelvis and sternum (breastbone) contain hollow air-filled cavities rather than marrow. This feature aids buoyancy and is an adaptation for flight. These air cavities link up with the air-sacs, another adaptation to improve

A Blue and yellow macaw (Ara ararauna) *with a companion green-winged macaw* (Ara chloroptera), *showing mutual preening as part of normal bonding behaviour. Those large, powerful beaks can crack nutshells and inflict a painful bite, yet can also perform surprisingly delicate and gentle tasks.*

Budgerigars (Melopsittacus undulatus) *demonstrating the large fleshy cere that these birds have, containing the nostrils. These pictures also show an idea of the range of colouring in this domesticated species: budgies are seen in many shades of blue, through violet, grey, shades of green, yellow and white. The blue bird is a mature male – its cere is bright blue. The green and yellow bird is a mature female in breeding condition – hens' ceres are normally brown, but there may be a slight flush of blue when hormone levels are high in the breeding season.*

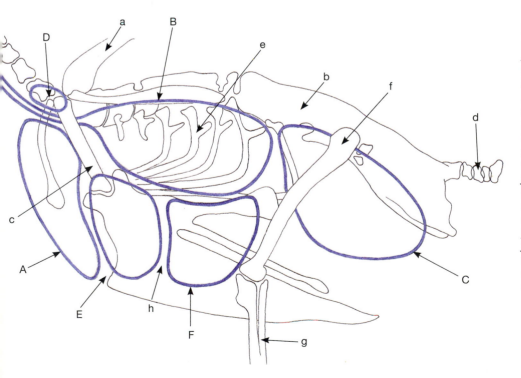

The respiratory and skeletal systems of a parrot. A=cervical air sac; B=lung; C=abdominal air sac; D=interclavicular air sac; E=anterior thoracic air sac; F=posterior thoracic air sac (upper case lettering represents the respiratory system of the bird, with interconnecting air sacs arising from the lungs).
a=humerus; b=pelvic bones; c=scapula; d=tail vertebrae; e=ribs with uncinate processes; f=femur; g=tibia/fibula; h=sternum (lower case lettering indicates some of the major bones of the skeleton).

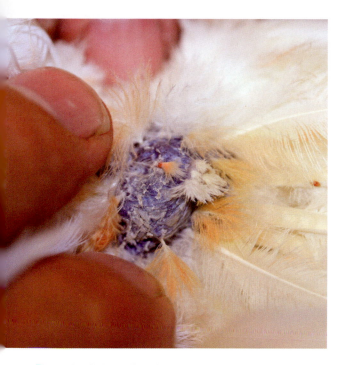

Preen gland above the tail-base of a Goffin's cockatoo (Cacatua goffini). The tuft of white feathers marks the duct where greasy secretion from this gland is exuded, and spread by the bird through its plumage.

Impacted preen gland in a budgerigar. The oily secretion has accumulated following blockage of the duct, resulting in swelling of the gland, secondary infection, and discomfort to the bird.

buoyancy and also to improve the efficiency of gas exchange in the respiratory system. There is *no* muscular diaphragm dividing the thorax from the abdomen. This inter-connection and unique respiratory system has clinical significance when it comes to diseases and will be discussed in more detail in Chapter 8.

The skin – both the dermis and epidermis – is thinner and more fragile than in mammals and reptiles. Basal cells produce both the horny keratin of the surface layer and oil droplets that coat the surface of the skin, providing waterproofing and anti-bacterial properties. Most also have a uropygial gland at the base of the spine just above the tail, which also produces an oily secretion aiding in plumage care and protection, as well as containing a precursor to vitamin D. This vitamin is converted on exposure to ultraviolet light, and is then ingested by the bird. This gland is not found in all parrots – it is notably absent in Amazons, Pionus and Brotogerys species.

Their kidneys are tri-lobed, and contain features common to both more primitive reptiles and more advanced mammalian systems. They produce a combined waste of liquid urine and semi-solid, crystalline white urates. These organs are closely applied to the pelvic bones, and many of the nerves pass through this area to the legs, with the consequence that inflammatory disease of the kidneys may damage these nerves, leading to paralysis of the legs. There is a renal portal system, whereby some 60 per cent of the blood flowing to the kidneys is supplied by veins from the back half of the body. This has important implications when it comes to injecting birds with medications.

The eyes of parrots are large, sensitive organs capable of detecting colour, including ultraviolet wavelengths. Being prey species, parrots have their eyes on the sides of their heads, to give a wider field of vision to look out for predators. The eyes are mobile, so that the bird may look down its beak at items held in its mouth, or upwards and

Yellow-naped Amazon (Amazona ochrocephala auropalliata) *exhibiting a threat display, with raised neck feathers and constricted pupils. The muscles of the iris in the eye are under voluntary control, and can be dilated and constricted by the bird at will. This bird is saying 'I do not want you to come any closer!' (Photo: Jan Hooimeijer DVM)*

backwards to search for danger. The muscles of the iris are striated, so parrots can voluntarily constrict and dilate their pupils. This action is used in threat display and courtship.

Inside the eye is the pecten, a black pleated structure with a rich blood supply, responsible for releasing nutrients into the vitreous. There is a third eyelid, or nictitating membrane, that will pass across the eye from the upper inner quadrant, releasing lubricating and cleaning secretions as it moves.

The above features are shared with all parrots. Species that are commonly kept in captivity are described in more detail in Chapter 3.

PLUMAGE

The feature that sets birds apart in the animal kingdom is not their ability to fly – there are flight-*less* birds, as well as mammals, reptiles and insects that can fly – but their possession of feathers. Parrots are no exception: there is one flightless species – the Kakapo from New Zealand – but all possess feathers. Above all it is the colour and arrangement of these feathers that has attracted man to parrot species. Feathers are highly complex structures, manufactured from the strong protein keratin, with a wide variety of functions.

Structure

There are several different types of feather found on a bird's body, and the proportions will vary according to species and lifestyle.

Contour feathers form the bulk of the plumage, and have the familiar appearance of a soft vane arising from a more rigid quill. The base of the quill without vanes is known as the calamus, while the upper section with feather vanes is the rachis. The young growing feather emerges from a follicle in the skin, and at this stage the quill has a nutrient blood supply with a network of capillary tissue in the base of the calamus. This shows through as a blue/pink fleshy colouration, and is known as a blood feather. This growth phase is uncomfortable for the bird, and is sensitive to dietary influences – temperature change, hormone levels or other stressors – which may damage the growing feather, resulting in stress bars.

The main shape and colourful section of the feather consists of the vane, formed by a system of barbs arising from the quill, which in turn have subsidiary interlocking barbules. This interlocking structure confers flexible strength coupled with lightness, and also waterproofing by virtue of its physical barrier and water-repellent properties. Preening is an essential activity carried out by the

Freddie, Green-cheeked conure (Pyrrhura molinae) *showing the nictitating membrane (third eyelid) passing across its eye. This membrane has a cleaning and protective function. Note also again the hooked bill, the nostrils in the cere, and the bald area around the eye, so typical of many parrot species.*

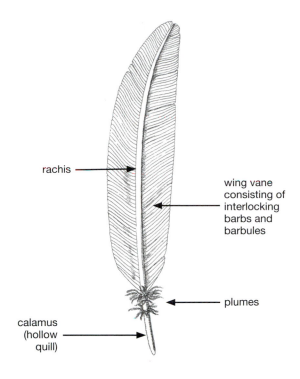

rachis

wing vane
consisting of
interlocking
barbs and
barbules

plumes

calamus
(hollow
quill)

Anatomy of a mature contour feather.

Contour feather from a parrot, showing the hollow, cylindrical quill. The shaft without coloured vanes is known as the calamus, and inserts into the bird's skin. The section with vanes is the rachis.

African grey parrot chick (Psittacus erithacus) showing new growth and development of wing feathers. Note the blue-grey shaft, full of rich blood supply – hence 'blood feathers'.

'Stress bars' in the tail feathers of a military macaw (Ara militaris). These result from some form of stressful event while the feather is developing in its sheath. Such things as temperature fluctuations, hormonal influences, or dietary imbalance will cause such reactions. (Photo: Jan Hooimeijer DVM)

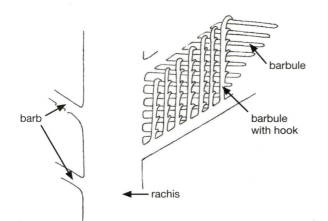

Detailed structure of barbs and barbules of a feather. Rigid barbs branch off each side of the central rachis. Branching off the barbs in turn are smaller barbules with hooked ends. These interlock with the barbules from the adjacent barb, rather like a Velcro® fastener. This interlocking action is a very effective method of providing rigidity and waterproofing, coupled with light weight. The preening action of the bird serves to re-attach barbule hooks that have become detached, thus maintaining the integrity of the plumage.

bird, to re-set barbules that become unzipped with activity.

The longest feathers on the bird are the flight feathers of the wings, where they are known as remiges, and in the tail, where they are called retrices. The remiges are asymmetrical, with the

BELOW: *A flight feather from a parrot (Remex, plural remiges). In these contour feathers, the leading edge of the wing has shorter vanes than the trailing edge, very much like an aeroplane's wing in profile.*

ABOVE: *A long tail feather from a parrot (Retrix, plural retrices). These are generally bilaterally symmetrical about the central quill, with vanes on each side being about equal in size.*

Body contour feathers. These are shorter than remiges and retrices, and have many more soft plumes at the junction of calamus and rachis.

ABOVE: *Cockatiel* (Nymphicus hollandicus) *showing the erectile crest feathers typical of this species. This bird is a male, having much brighter orange and yellow colouring on his cheeks than does a female.*

leading edge having shorter vanes than the trailing edge, and in profile they have an aerofoil shape. The retrices, on the other hand, are bilaterally symmetrical about the quill. Smaller contour feathers cover most of the bird's body, upper legs, and bases of the wings.

Modified contour feathers are seen as erectile or permanent crests in species such as the cockatiel (*Nymphicus hollandicus*) or the cockatoo. Some contour feathers may be minute, like the blue 'eyelashes' surrounding the eye of the hen Eclectus parrot. The facial lines in macaws are rows of small contour feathers, almost as individual as fingerprints.

Contour feathers are replaced at a regular moulting cycle as they wear out – see below.

Down feathers have more of an insulating function, so their barbules do not interlock but remain loose (plumulaceous, compared with interlocked

RIGHT: *Oscar again, citron-crested cockatoo* (Cacatua sulphurea citrinocristata) *showing the erectile crest feathers used in display and to show emotional responses like anger, fear, or excitement.*

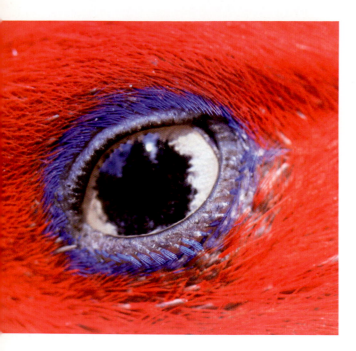

LEFT: *The eye of a female Eclectus parrot: the minute blue 'eyelashes' look as if they have been carefully brushed with eye shadow, but are in fact tiny contour feathers.*

pennaceous vanes). This allows a layer of air to be trapped in their substance. They are found under the outer layer of contour feathers on the body, and – being fragile – are shed and replaced continuously throughout the life of the bird.

ABOVE: *Anatomy of a down feather. Down feathers have a rachis shorter than the longest barb, or it may be absent altogether. There are numerous barbs with non-interlocking barbules.*

LEFT: *The facial lines in this green-winged macaw (*Ara chloroptera*) are also minute contour feathers, while the pattern of lines is almost as individual to the bird as are human fingerprints. A photograph of your macaw may well prove to be a useful identity feature in claims of disputed ownership, if the bird should be lost or stolen and then retrieved.*

'Ari', a Lesser Sulphur-crested cockatoo (Cacatua sulphurea sulphurea) with advanced Psittacine Beak and Feather Disease (PBFD). The soft feathers on her flank are powder-down feathers, which fragment continually, shedding a fine dust that is spread by the bird throughout its plumage to act as a conditioner.

Powder-down feathers are short, soft, brush-shaped feathers over the flanks, designed to break up into a fine powder used by the bird as a grooming aid and dry lubricant.

More specialized modified feathers are found in the form of display plumes in birds like the peacock (*Pavo* spp.) or crowned crane (*Balearica regulorum*). In parrots, there may be bristles, for example in the Kakapo (*Strigops habroptilus*).

Colour

All the bird's feathers together make up its plumage, and the majority of parrot species have very colourful plumage, a big part of their attraction to humans. Their varied shape and bright colours make them highly prized for use as ceremonial accessories in many groups of people around the world.

Some parrot types are predominantly one full colour – for example the white cockatoos. Closer examination reveals the underside of feathers to be suffused with yellow in *Cacatua alba*, the Umbrella cockatoo or pink in the Moluccan

RIGHT: *Crowned crane* (Balearica regulorum) *showing specialized feathers forming a plume-display on its head.*

ABOVE: *Umbrella cockatoo* (Cacatua alba) *showing yellow suffusion of predominantly white feathers.*

cockatoo (*Cacatua moluccensis*), Goffin's cockatoo (*Cacatua goffini*), or Leadbeater's cockatoo (*Cacatua leadbeateri*). Crest feathers may be pink in the Moluccan cockatoo, or shades of yellow or orange, or red white and yellow. Black cockatoos come with white, yellow or red tail feathers, and even the all-black palm cockatoo (*Probosciger aterrimus*) has plumage with a colourful sheen or gradation of shade.

Most other parrots have multiple feather colours in various combinations and distribution over the body, with the aptly named Rainbow lory (*Trichoglossus haematodus*) being a good example. The close-up of the Australian king parakeet (*Alisterus scapularis*) shows red green and blue feathers in close proximity. Even the grey body colour of the African grey, or the green of the Amazons, is – on closer inspection – made up with individual feathers with scalloped colouring.

Colour is provided in two distinct ways – pigment and structure. *Pigment-based colours* may be melanins, showing as blacks, browns and some yellows; carotenoids, producing reds, oranges

LEFT: *The striking Moluccan cockatoo* (Cacatua moluccensis) *with pink feather colouration.*

Goffin's cockatoo (Cacatua goffini), *a bird with predominantly white plumage, but with pink patches. Note also the area of bald skin around the eye, typical of many cockatoos.*

ABOVE: *Leadbeater's (or Major Mitchell's) cockatoo* (Cacatua leadbeateri) *with under-wing feathers deep pink in colour.*

BELOW: *Crest feathers of Leadbeater's cockatoo, showing the distinctive bands of red, yellow and white.*

LEFT: *Black palm cockatoo* (Probosciger aterrimus) *with all black feathers, but with variable gradation of colour and sheen. Note the large upper beak and the relaxed crest feathers (compare with the erect crest shown in the photograph on pages 9 and 19), as well as the cheek feathers extending up over the mandible – something that these birds do when relaxed. The bare skin on the cheeks will vary from pale pink, if the bird is asleep or unwell, to bright red when active and excited.*

Rainbow lories (Trichoglossus haematodus) in a bird park taking nectar from a visitor's cup. Note the variety and colour of the feathers in these birds.

Even the grey plumage of the African grey parrot shows scalloped edges to the feathers with different shades of grey.

ABOVE: *Rump of the Australian king parakeet* (Alisterus scapularis) *showing red, green and blue feathers in close proximity. Red and green are pigmented colours; blue is a structural colour.*

and some yellows; or porphyrins responsible for some greens and reds. All these pigments are complex molecules, produced by the liver, and liver malfunction or dietary deficiency will manifest in abnormal plumage colouring, such as yellow patches in the normal green of an Amazon parrot or pink patches in the grey parrot.

Structural colour is provided by the refraction or reflection of light through the semi-transparent keratin tissue of the feather and the air trapped within it. Totally reflected light will show as white: white feathers contain no pigment molecules at all

ABOVE: *Primrose-cheeked or Red-lored Amazon parrot* (Amazona autumnalis) *Nelson, showing abnormal yellow feathers scattered through the green. The beak and claws are also overgrown. These changes are the result of liver disease in this bird, with a consequent lack of protein for feather pigment.*

and are structurally weaker than pigmented types. This may be a contributory factor in the frequency of feather problems in white cockatoos. 'Mirrored' reflected wavelengths will produce an iridescent

LEFT: *Blue fronted Amazon* (Amazona aestiva), *like most Amazon parrots, has largely green plumage with variable distribution of other colours. However, like the grey parrot, each body feather has a scalloped border of a different shade of green.*

African grey parrot showing unusual pink feathers among the grey. This may be a transient phase in many juvenile birds, as proteins are used quickly in rapid growth. These birds generally moult out and replace the pink with grey as the bird matures. More persistent pink feathering can indicate protein deficiency or liver disease, or in some cases the early stages of psittacine beak and feather disease (PBFD). Occasionally we see abnormal colour mutations with varying amounts of pink or red feathers over the body – so-called King Jockos. Finally, the appearance of pink feathers in a bird that persistently plucks its feathers indicates a depletion of protein reserves or permanent damage to the feather follicle, thereby affecting its development.

CASE STUDY: NELSON'S FEATHERS

The green parrot pictured here and on page 25 is Nelson, a red-lored or primrose-cheeked Amazon *Amazona autumnalis*), which was presented to my clinic by a representative of a parrot rescue and rehabilitation group. His previous owners had grown tired of him, and he had lived a life confined to a small cage with no freedom, and fed a diet of human junk food, including pizza, chips and kebabs! His beak and claws were overgrown and misshapen, while the plumage was dotted with the yellow feathers seen in the first picture.

Examination and blood sampling revealed an overweight bird with degenerative liver disease. Appropriate treatment and attention to his diet produced a slow, steady improvement in body condition, general health, beak and claw growth, and plumage. Gradually, as he went through successive moults, the abnormal yellow feathers were replaced with properly pigmented green feathers, as the liver recovered and produced normal pigmentation. Ten years later, Nelson still comes in to see me for the occasional claw clip, but is a much better looking bird!

Nelson ten years on, following earlier treatment for his liver condition. Now showing plumage of a normal colour, with a healthy sheen.

sheen of green, blue, or violet in bright light; while the 'Tyndall effect' is a scattering of light particles within the feather structure, reflecting just blue wavelengths. Most blue colouring in parrot feathers is the result of this effect.

Some colours result from a mix of structure and pigment – thus yellow pigment granules plus blue scatter show as green.

Body feathers on a blue pennant parakeet (Platycercus elegans *mutation*). *The grey/black is due to the presence of melanin pigment; the white edges are parts of the feather that structurally reflect all wavelengths of light; while the blue areas partly scatter and partly reflect blue wavelengths (the Tyndall effect).*

A pair of Eclectus parrots. These birds are unusual in the parrot family for their marked sexual dimorphism: hen birds are predominantly red, with blue, violet, and some yellow feathers. Their beaks are all black. Cock birds are predominantly green in colour, with touches of blue or red on flanks and wing edges, while their beaks are orange/yellow.

Plumage colour may be used to identify species or sex of the bird. Obvious differences make the African grey parrot easy to identify against a Blue and yellow macaw (*Ara ararauna*); more subtle distinctions are noted within the various Amazon and lory/lorikeet species and their (often disputed) sub-species (*see* Chapter 3). As stated above, some parrots are sexually dimorphic – that is males and females are visibly different – the most obvious example being the Eclectus parrots. Males in this group are generally green, while females are mostly red. This subject will be amplified in more detail later, but we do know that birds are capable of visualizing ultraviolet light as well as our 'visible' spectrum, so it is quite likely that they see visual differences between their sexes that we cannot.

A blue-fronted Amazon parrot (Amazona aestiva) *as humans see it – predominantly green, with red wing-flashes, and variable areas of Blue and yellow around the head. Sexes appear to us identical in physical appearance.*

Because parrots are capable of visualizing ultraviolet wavelengths of light, this is how the same bird might appear to its companions. It is quite possible that UV reflection would be different for each sex, so the birds can see an obvious visible difference in males and females.

Feather colour may also indicate the age of the bird, as many species have a juvenile or adolescent plumage, preceding that of the sexually mature adult. The ring-necked parakeets (*Psittacula* species – *see* Chapter 3) are good examples. Yellow-headed Amazons tend to develop more yellow on their heads with maturity. Young African grey parrots have grey-tipped red tail feathers, which moult out at about one year old to be replaced with pure red.

Colour is used by parrots in display – over territory, in courtship and breeding, in fear or aggression. Wings will be raised or tails spread, showing flashes of bright red or orange; vivid chest feathers may be raised with the underlying flesh inflated; or colourful crest feathers may be raised and lowered. Many bird species use plumage colour in camouflage, especially in nesting hens or precocial chicks, but this is rarely the case in parrots.

Function

Feathers have a number of important functions. The most obvious of these is *flight,* although as previously stated, this property is not unique to birds. The muscles, nerves and tendons serving the long flight feathers and the skeleton of the wings control the movements of these limbs, while the

A Blue and yellow macaw (Ara ararauna) *used in a public flying display at a bird park, demonstrating how it uses its tail feathers as an air-break when landing.*

strong but flexible structure of the feathers enables them to provide lift, reduce drag, and act rather like ailerons on an aeroplane. The tail feathers are used as rudders and air brakes.

The second function is *insulation*. The plumage holds within its structure a quantity of air that is warmed by body heat and retained by the feathers. Cold or sick birds 'fluff up' their feathers to increase the depth of this layer of air, while hot birds will pant and raise their feathers to release trapped air. Birds have no sweat glands in their skin.

Thirdly, feathers are responsible for *waterproofing*. This is achieved primarily by the unique interlocking properties of the feather barbules, which when properly in place create a surface impermeable to water droplets. This is aided by the naturally water-repellent properties of the structural keratin, supported by an oily secretion from the preen gland spread through the plumage as the bird preens. However, not all parrots have preen glands – Amazons and Pionus for example – yet all are waterproof, so the protective effects of this gland are often over-emphasized.

It is clear therefore that both insulation and waterproofing will be severely compromised if the delicate feather structure is damaged. Lack of preening by the bird, oily or greasy deposits on the plumage, poor growth because of dietary deficiencies or liver disease, damage from external parasites or infectious diseases, or a hot dry atmosphere with no facility to bathe – all will deleteriously affect this delicate material. Results will include heat loss, skin irritation and infection, over-preening leading to feather-plucking, and a general decline in the bird's condition.

Finally, plumage is used in *display*, as mentioned above. Erectile muscles in the skin are under voluntary control of the bird, to raise and lower feathers at will, showing particular patches of colour or formation.

Moulting

The delicate structure of feathers means that they will wear out in time, and have to be replaced. Down or powder-down feathers are replaced continually, but contour feathers are replaced in a regular process known as the moult. This replacement process is also used in birds that have a seasonal plumage, such as ptarmigan (*Lagopus muta*), but this rarely applies to parrots. In general, the major moult takes place after the breeding season, once the birds have carried out their annual peak function and can 'sit back' to recover. The moulting process itself is draining in terms of energy and nutrients, with some 30 per cent increase in metabolic energy required. Extra essential amino acids are required to manufacture the proteins required for the formation of keratin and pigments; calcium is an essential mineral needed for the process.

Old feathers loosen in their follicles, and incipient new growth occurs at the 'germinal bud' at the base of the follicle. Parrots spend more time resting and preening – this is an irritating period for the bird, and is often the first stage of a plucking problem. Humidity and bathing are more important at this time – dry heat will make feathers brittle and even more itchy. The full length and weight of the feather shaft is important to stimulate the moulting process, thus wing feathers that have been clipped will often be retained, causing further irritation to the bird and again predisposing to plucking.

Birds that are kept indoors, with artificial photoperiod, dry warm atmosphere, and no facility to breed, will usually shed their feathers year-round, rather than for a defined period. This also will lead to an increase in feather-plucking behaviour in pet indoor birds compared with their outdoor-dwelling cousins.

Ducks and geese have an 'eclipse moult', when all their fight feathers are moulted at one time, rendering them temporarily flightless. Parrots on the other hand shed their flight feathers sequentially and in bilaterally symmetrical pairs, so they still retain the power of flight. Gaps will appear in the wing where the old feather is lost and before the new one reaches full size, but this is never enough to prevent flight.

The new feather is encased in a keratin 'sheath', and is known as a 'blood feather' because of its rich capillary network supplying nutrients within the calamus. This sheath is progressively shed as a powdery 'dandruff' as the feather grows and unfurls, and the blood supply shrinks back, to eventually leave the hollow quill of the mature feather. The blood feather is soft and vulnerable, and if damaged will bleed profusely. Should such an accident occur, the best remedy is to grasp the base of the shaft, and pull it completely out with a twist and pull action. The small arteriole supplying the feather will recoil like a rubber band, and quickly seal: a new feather will grow soon afterwards. Attempts to repair or cauterize the bleeding broken quill will usually result in the bird worrying at the scab and encouraging fresh haemorrhage; repeated episodes may lead to feather infection and damage to the follicle.

A decorative stained-glass panel depicting a stylized parrot, demonstrating how much these birds are appreciated for their colour and form by humans.

CHAPTER 2

Choosing the Right Parrot

Purchasing a parrot should never be an impulse buy! Rescue centres are full to bursting with unwanted birds passed on by owners who cannot cope with their demands.

WHAT CAN GO WRONG?

Parrots are long-lived and intelligent, and have physical and mental needs that many owners find they are unable to fulfil. So many times in my practice I have met owners who have been seduced by the cuddly, silly-tame, baby cockatoo in the pet store. These birds, almost without exception, grow into demanding, screeching, destructive, and even aggressive adults. They are mentally uncertain whether to be human children or parrots – more of that later.

Large macaws are noisy and need a lot of space; *Aratinga* conures are extremely raucous for their size. Neither group is suited to suburban living in close proximity to neighbours who will soon protest against the persistent noise.

Dougal, Umbrella cockatoo (Cacatua alba) *screaming and raising his wings to demonstrate that he is having his personal space invaded and does not like it. If the threat persists and he cannot escape, then he will do the only thing left to protect himself and attack the approaching animal or person.*

People hear that the ideal talking parrot is the African grey *(Psittacus erithacus)*, but these also are prone to psychological and behavioural problems, including feather-plucking, and very often turn out to be 'one-person' birds. They will bond to one member of the household, and will ignore – or even actively attack – other people in the family.

Anyone who likes a pristine, neat and tidy home will have great difficulty in achieving that objective with pets in the house, and that is particularly so if you keep a parrot. They scatter their food in

A pair of cockatoos on their play-stand in a living room. In this situation they will scatter their food, droppings, feather dust and debris from their toys around the room. Note the selection of rope and wooden toys and the cardboard roll and box for them to chew. Note also the air filter beside the fireplace, used to reduce the amount of atmospheric dust shed by the birds. (The fire is not working – it would pose a hazard if it were.) There are, however, loose wires, candles, books and magazines all in easy reach of the birds and inviting their curiosity. Such items will at least be seriously damaged by the parrots, and at worst could prove hazardous to the birds.

ABOVE: *A pair of Sun conures* (Aratinga solstitialis). *These are colourful and playful birds, but extremely noisy, and are not recommended if you want a quiet life or have close neighbours! These two birds have just enjoyed a bath, and are preening their plumage, something that healthy parrots spend a lot of time doing.*

BELOW: *African grey parrot Eric, probably the most popular of the larger parrots, because of their renowned talking ability. However, they are subject to many psychological and behavioural problems if not properly understood and cared for.*

all directions – and splashes of pomegranate juice up the walls are difficult to remove! They release fine feather dust into the atmosphere. The worst offenders in this regard are cockatiels, cockatoos and African grey parrots.

Scattered seed-husks and feather dust; high pitched screeches and whistles while you are trying to watch your favourite TV programme; possible illnesses that may develop; and the need for alternative carers when you go away – these may all influence your attitude to pet parrots.

Best for Children

Parrots are not pets to buy for a child on a whim. Young children should be introduced to the joys and responsibilities of pet-keeping with a gerbil, hamster, or mouse. Serious commitment to short-lived pets like these could then allow progression to a budgerigar or cockatiel. Experience gained in the management of these 'easier' species is an essential prerequisite to better care of larger, longer-lived, and more demanding parrots.

A cockatiel (Nymphicus hollandicus) *is recommended as a first-time, comparatively easily cared-for small parrot. However, even these can be noisy, they are dusty, and hen birds can be prolific egg-layers.*

A Senegal parrot (Poicephalus senegalus), *one of the small, family-friendly, comparatively trouble-free parrots recommended as a pet bird.*

If you are certain that you wish to take on a parrot, then you have to decide on the species. If you have young children you will need a gentle, tolerant bird that will accept handling, noise, and the general bustle of family life.

At the same time, its lifespan is important. Children grow up and lose interest in what was once an all-consuming passion, and they leave home sooner or later. It is the parents that then get left with the responsibility! Again we come back to the choice of a budgerigar, cockatiel, or perhaps small *Poicephalus* parrots like a Meyer's *(P. meyeri)* or a Senegal *(P. senegalus)* There is, however, no denying that the importance to a child of taking responsibility and caring for a pet is an invaluable part of their education for life.

POINTS TO CONSIDER

The Environment You Can Offer

Think of the space available in your home. There would be little point in taking on a large hyacinthine or green-winged macaw in a one-bedroomed apartment, but a large sprawling farmhouse could accommodate several such birds.

Think of the neighbours and the sound-proofing of your house. If you live in the middle of nowhere, you could keep as many noisy birds as you wish, but all the parrot family have noise potential, and semi-detached or terraced suburbia is not the best place for such pets. You will undoubtedly receive complaints about noise sooner or later. Even if you and the birds lived there first, new neighbours can and will complain after they have moved in, if noise is excessive and repetitive. Such precautions as double-glazing, heavy curtains, thick walls, and a reasonable lifestyle where the birds are put to bed (by covering the cages or placing them in a darkened room) and woken up at an acceptable hour are paramount.

If you are opting for garden aviaries to house your parrots, then you really will have to address the noise issue, with trees or shrubs to screen the flights, and pop-holes to keep the birds inside their sleeping quarters until well after dawn.

Costs

Think of the costs involved. There is not just the initial price of the bird, but you will need the largest cage you can afford and accommodate, plus possibly a travelling cage and a sleeping cage as well. Your bird will need to be fed properly, and this will include quality food, with fresh fruit and vegetables, and probably avian-specific nutritional supplements. The parrot will need toys to interest and stimulate him. These can be cheap and home-made, but there is a large market of expensive wooden, rope and plastic parrot toys available, that can be destroyed by that powerful beak in a very short time.

There may be veterinary costs as well – perhaps just the occasional check-up with a wing or nail trim; or maybe more serious illness, injury or accident that could incur expensive specialist fees.

A varied selection of rope and wooden toys available for parrots, also incorporating chains and such items as coconut shells. There is a large market in such toys, but it is necessary to ensure that they are coloured only with safe vegetable dyes, and that the chains are of stainless steel and not galvanized metal.

Then there are holidays or illness: who do you get to look after your bird(s) while you are away, or ill, and how much will it cost? Boarding kennels and catteries for dogs and cats are commonplace, but parrot-boarding or bird-sitters are not so easy to find.

HOW OLD IS IT?

Novice parrot-keepers may choose an African grey parrot, as they want a 'good talker', and they have heard that a baby bird is ideal for this purpose. They will seek out the pet shop with the cheapest specimens, and find a bird cowering at the back of its cage, growling when approached.

If they ever get close enough to the bird to check it out, they may notice that its eyes have yellow irises. Experienced parrot keepers will know that a juvenile grey parrot (as do most macaws) have a grey-coloured iris which starts to turn yellow at about one year old, becoming increasingly yellow with age. So the prospective purchaser should be looking for such a grey-eyed baby – but because they have not researched the subject properly may not be aware of that fact.

The store owner, anxious for a quick sale, will say something like, 'Oh, he's just a little upset, he'll settle fine when you get him home,' and will swear blind that the bird is just the baby specimen the customer is looking for.

Now of course it may be that the seller is as ignorant of normal parrot characteristics as is the buyer (and believe me, that is not impossible – in which case, why are they selling birds?). But sadly the usual scenario is that the seller is simply taking advantage of the customer's naivety. This is not an isolated case: I have seen many examples of such an occurrence in my career.

Juvenile African grey parrot with a grey iris. This grey colouration is present during the first ten to twelve months, and starts to turn yellow from one year old. The intensity of the yellow increases until the bird is about five years old, and then stays unchanged. The same is true of macaws.

Adult African grey parrot showing the yellow colour of the iris of his eye.

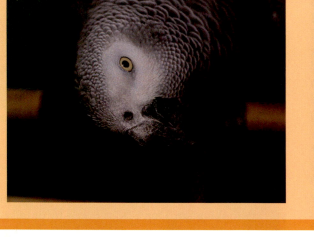

water and little food, possibly feather-plucked – and decide to 'rescue it' from its appalling conditions. Both these purchases are potentially fraught with long-term disaster, ongoing expense, and heartache.

If you do choose a bird from a pet store, select a shop that specializes in birds, and has their parrots kept in a separate bird room in the premises. This will reduce stress on the birds, as well as cutting down on the spread of infectious diseases, while ensuring that only those customers actively interested in purchase are allowed access by the staff.

Bird rooms in pet stores, separate from the main shop area, well-lit, secure, giving the birds room to play and interact with each other. Staff will allow only customers genuinely interested in purchasing a parrot into this area, thereby reducing the risk of spreading infection and stress to the birds.

The ideal situation is to find a reputable supplier, see your chosen bird, handle it and examine it, then pay a deposit, and come back again to review your potential purchase. Then when you finally commit to buying, do so on the understanding that you may have it vet-checked within five days, and a full money-back guarantee for any pre-existing health problems that manifest within ten days. At this point, many retailers will offer temporary insurance cover. It is important to pursue this option and take out annual insurance as soon as you can.

What to Look for

The purchaser should look for an alert, active bird, which is bright-eyed, with no signs of ocular (eye) or nasal discharge. Feathers should be sleek and shiny, with none seriously frayed or missing. Many young birds will have ragged edges to some wing or tail feathers where they have been caged. This is not a major problem, and more space, regular bathing, and the first moult will result in improved plumage condition.

Frayed tail feathers in a white cockatoo, resulting from persistent clinging to the bars of a cage, so that the tail rubs against the wire.

Food and water bowls and the cage of a pet-shop parrot. Check to see that the food and water are fresh and clean, that the bird has been eating, and that the cage and perches are clean. Look at the droppings in the cage, or for signs of vomiting or sneezing.

Normal droppings of an average parrot. The waste product consists of a coil of faeces, coloured dark green or almost black, depending on the diet. Here the coil to the right is paler in colour, following the ingestion of fruit (apple and orange). Examination of this part of the droppings would give an indication of bowel health in the bird. The second component is bright white urates, a semi-solid material eliminated from the kidneys. Outside that is a liquid urine fraction which will vary in quantity according to the bird's diet – nectar feeders like lories and lorikeets pass more urine than seed-eaters. Grapes, oranges or apples in the diet will result in paler, more liquid droppings. Diseases such as kidney problems or diabetes will dramatically increase the volume of urine passed.

Stand and observe the bird for several minutes to allow it to relax. Watch for signs of excessive preening or scratching; favouring one leg or wing; closing of eyes or sneezing and coughing. Look at the food and water bowls – firstly, are they clean and is the food of good quality? Secondly, has the bird been eating?

Look for a messy vent –the area under the tail may be clogged with droppings stuck to the feathers – and check the droppings themselves. They should be firm, and generally a mixture of bright white urates with dark green or black faeces. Birds fed a pelleted diet or a large percentage of

Feathers around the vent of a bird soiled with sticky droppings. This would indicate a digestive disorder, or a bird that is spending prolonged periods on the floor rather than perching.

vegetable will have a browner faecal component, and foods like cherries, strawberries, blackberries, chillies or beetroot will colour the droppings. Very liquid faeces, smelly droppings, spots of blood, or very green or yellow urates should ring alarm bells. Signs of vomit – either on the cage floor or around the bird's face – should also be cause for concern.

The beak should be well-aligned and not overgrown or excessively flaky. A crumbly, brittle appearance, with a broad tip to the upper beak, can indicate vitamin or mineral deficiency; fungal infection in the beak tissue; or liver disease in older birds. 'Scissor beak' is a lateral deviation, common in macaws and cockatoos, that at least will require frequent trimming, and in more severe cases may need surgical correction.

Watch the bird move around the cage. Does it use both legs and its beak to climb successfully, and does it perch comfortably and normally with both feet? Does it stretch and spread both wings

ABOVE: *Droppings showing sparse faecal material, indicating that the bird is eating little, and very green-stained urates. This is indicative of liver or kidney disease, very often linked to psittacosis.*

'Scissor beak' in a young Scarlet macaw (Ara macao), where the upper beak deviates to one side. This is most commonly the result of nutritional deficiencies or congenital abnormalities, but may also follow injury to the growing tissue; persistent running of the beak up and down cage wire; or possibly the use of a syringe for feeding baby birds, inserted persistently on the same side of the mouth – although this latter reason is unlikely.

BELOW: *An overgrown, flaky beak in a yellow budgerigar. This is generally a reflection of chronic dietary deficiencies or liver disease.*

Surgical correction of scissor beak using a metal and wire brace to pull the upper beak back into alignment. The older the bird and the more deviation there is of the beak, the less effective such techniques are likely to be.

Severely mutilated wing feathers on a young parrot following an excessive and early wing clip. The cut quills have irritated the bird, so it has proceeded to chew the cut ends.

Self-mutilation in a chronically plucked cockatoo. These birds will progress from feather pulling to breaking through the skin and muscle. At this stage the bird will be debilitated from blood loss and the condition can be very difficult to cure.

equally and normally? Can it fly if allowed out of the cage? Many suppliers will routinely wing-clip young birds before sale, often younger than twelve weeks – 'to make it easier to tame and handle the bird'. Avoid such birds, or refuse to agree to wing-clipping if it is offered as an option. Such birds will not yet have learned how to take off, fly, and land successfully, and may injure themselves in consequence. They certainly will be frustrated, and (especially young grey parrots and cockatoos) may start to pick at the cut quills and progress to serious feather-plucking or self-mutilation.

Handling the parrot when possible should enable one to assess its temperament and bodyweight. The breast muscles should be rounded, with the sternum (keel bone) just visible as a central ridge. If these muscles are severely wasted, there is a long-term health problem. In older birds, if the muscles would make Dolly Parton proud, then the bird is obese! This is a particular problem in galah (roseate) cockatoos (*Eolophus roseicapillus*), some white cockatoos and older pet Amazon parrots.

Umbrella cockatoo Dougal again. His chronic plucking reveals his nicely rounded pectoral muscles on either side of the sternum (keel bone). Note also the zygodactyl toes – two forward and two back – typical of parrots.

A Bourke's parakeet (Neophema bourkii) submitted for post-mortem examination. In this case the breast muscles are severely wasted, exposing the sternum. However, until the feathers are plucked from it, this is not so obvious in the live bird. They will fluff out their plumage and appear fit and well for as long as they can.

ABOVE: *Overweight Galah cockatoo (Eolophus roseicapillus), a common problem in these birds. The feathers disguise the fact somewhat, but the abdominal area is still clearly enlarged.*

BELOW: *This Citron-crested cockatoo Maxi, because she has feather-plucked, more clearly shows bulging fat deposits over her lower abdomen and thighs. Note also the orangey-red colour of the iris, indicating that this bird is a hen. Compare with the dark brown or black iris of the cock bird on pages 9 and 19.*

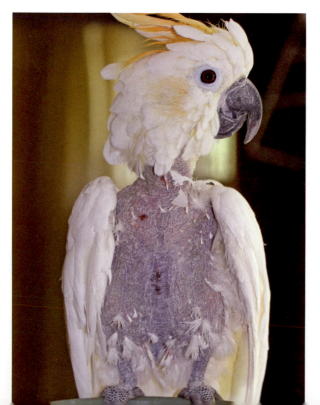

Buying for Breeding?

Purchasing birds for breeding or outside aviaries is a whole different ball game. The same criteria of bright-eyes, good plumage and attitude apply, but here one is usually purchasing adult birds in pairs or more.

Again, it is easy to find cheap birds in on-line or newspaper adverts, but ask yourself why the birds are so cheap? The bird-keeping world includes some very interesting, honest, caring and friendly people, but sadly also more than its fair share of rogues. Sellers will say that they are getting rid of their stock to move house, change lifestyle, or because of ill-health, marriage break-up or death of a partner, or to change bird species – all of which may be true, and certainly will sound plausible.

However – *caveat emptor* again – these tales have also been used by breeders wishing to pass on their old stock, egg-eaters or chick killers, infertile or incompatible pairs, or even diseased birds. Slowly incubating infections like PBFD, PDD or psittacosis (*see* pages 162–167) can take months to manifest, so unscrupulous owners may sell knowingly-infected birds on the open market. This action brings heartache and expense to the new owner, as well as disseminating these unpleasant diseases. Potential purchasers should therefore once again check that the source is reliable, and ask for certificates for disease testing, sex, age and identity (tattoo, microchip or leg ring).

A closed leg ring (band) on a parrot. This one is made of aluminium: the 99 refers to the year of hatch, and therefore indicates the bird's age. The HP would be the breeder's initials, and the number 8 is just the eighth ring of that size used by that breeder in 1999. This ring would have been slipped over the foot of the bird while still a chick in the nest. Split rings may be applied later in life, using special pliers, and may indicate the sex of the bird, following endoscopy or DNA analysis. These may be made of stainless steel or aluminium. Plastic rings are also used for identification, but are obviously less durable.

CHAPTER 3

Common Captive Parrots

Fashions change in bird-keeping, as with any other branch of livestock. Far fewer parrots are imported from the wild these days, so availability of some species has changed. Some species are difficult to breed in captivity, so stocks are not regenerated, while others may be bred but are not easy to sell because of waning popularity. This is true of lories and lorikeets, once widespread in breeding collections, but now falling out of favour because of their demanding husbandry and dietary requirements. Amongst the smaller species – budgerigars, cockatiels and grass parakeets – there is an increasing desire to breed mutation colour varieties (especially in mainland Europe), while the pure original type reduces in numbers. Hyacinthine macaws and black cockatoos are more readily available and more numerous in the USA than in Europe.

What follows is by no means an exhaustive catalogue of the wide variety of parrot species, but describes a selection of the popular types found in captivity at the time of writing. A book of this type written ten years ago would have included species not mentioned here. The same written ten years hence (in whatever format it may appear!) is likely to give yet another list. Approximate sizes and life-expectancy are given where possible, to aid your choice of parrot. Longevity is the expected average: there are always exceptions to every rule, with some very long-lived parrots about, as well as those that sadly die young.

SMALL PARAKEETS

Budgerigars *(Melopsittacus undulatus)*

Perhaps the most popular and familiar of the small parakeets, and probably the closest we have to a 'domesticated species', this little bird is native of dry, temperate grasslands in Australia, where they gather in huge, noisy flocks. The wild bird is small – total length about 18cm, half of which is tail, with bodyweight about 30gm. Its feathers are primarily green, with a yellow head, and the dorsal plumage is distinctively scalloped.

From this original native stock, almost two hundred years of captive breeding and selection have produced a much larger (25cm and 35–50gm), rounder bird, with a multitude of colour varieties. There are even crested strains. Feathers of the back and wings retain the scalloped appearance, and juvenile birds have 'bars' across

An aviary containing two of the many colour varieties of modern captive budgerigars (Melopsittacus undulatus).

Two young budgerigars – the blue and white bird shows black and white barring of the feathers across the forehead right down to the cere. The slightly older green and yellow bird has lost this feature, but both birds still have black eyes and lilac ceres, indicative of immature birds.

Adult budgerigar, with no barring on forehead and light-coloured iris in the eye.

the forehead, which disappear as the bird matures. In common with many parrots, iris colour also changes with age, being black in the youngsters and creamy-white in adults. There are distinctive dark spots on the plumage of the lower face. Sex differentiation in most adult birds is obvious by the colour of the large fleshy cere, containing the nostrils. This is blue in the male and brown in the female, but is a neutral lilac in juvenile birds and many of the paler colour mutations.

These birds are bright, active, intelligent, and make ideal small pet birds, or undemanding aviary specimens. There is a huge interest in breeding and showing budgerigars around the world. They will successfully mimic bells and whistles, and will learn to repeat many human words. They are highly sociable, so should ideally be kept at least in pairs, if not small groups. Indoors in captivity they are very prone to obesity. Budgerigars are also highly susceptible to tumours of many varieties and organ systems.

The average pet budgie can live for twelve to fifteen years, if of a green or blue colour. The more unusual colours such as yellow, white, violet or spangled tend to be less robust, and may last only seven to nine years. The more highly-bred show and breeding specimens may be old at five! Of course there are always exceptions, and I have encountered the occasional twenty-year-old bird.

Cockatiels *(Nymphicus hollandicus)*

Like the budgerigar, the cockatiel originates from Australia, but has also been kept in captivity for so many generations and with so many colour varieties bred in this time that these birds should be considered as domesticated species. Total length approaches 30cm. The 'normal grey' bird has a predominantly grey body with a yellow head and bright orange cheek-patches in the male. The hen is duller in facial colouring, and has yellow striations of the under-tail feathering. Years of captive breeding have now produced birds that are white-faced, all white, lutino (yellow) pied and pearl feathering. Their spiky crest feathers are their most distinctive feature.

Adult normal grey male cockatiel (Nymphicus hollandicus), *showing the bright yellow and orange head colouring, and the distinctive long crest feathers.*

Lutino cockatiel with yellow feathering.

These again are bright, characterful birds, and make ideal pets or easy aviary birds. They are noisier than budgerigars, with a shrill, repetitive call. They are strong fliers and prolific breeders, capable of producing fertile eggs at less than one year old. In fact it can be very difficult to stop these birds laying eggs! In a colony system they should be allowed equal-sized nest boxes, with more boxes available than there are breeding pairs, otherwise they will fight over the favoured choice of box.

In common with African grey parrots and cockatoos, they appear to produce far more dust from their plumage than do most other parrots. Average lifespan of the normal grey birds should easily reach fifteen to twenty, or even twenty-five years, but, as with budgies, the mutation colour varieties are less robust, and may make no more than ten to fifteen years.

Grass Parakeets (*Neophema* species)

Many species of this genus of Australian parakeets are popular in aviculture, mostly as aviary breeding birds rather than caged pet birds. Like cockatiels and budgerigars, they have been 'mucked about' with over several generations to produce a variety of colour mutations to the point where original

specimens of the nominate race are now rare. Such mutation forms are currently highly popular in Western Europe, and command high prices. They are short-bodied, long-tailed birds (about 20cm, weighing 40–60gm), with a small head and beak. Most are highly coloured, with variation between the sexes. Popular species include the Bourke's parakeet *(Neophema bourkii)*, the Splendid parakeet *(N. splendida)*, the Turquoisine *(N. pulchella)* and the Elegant parakeet *(N. elegans)*.

Lutino mutation of the Turquoisine Parakeet (Neophema pulchella). *The normal specimen has a green back and yellow belly, with blue on the wings and face.*

Pink mutation (Rosa) of the Bourke's parakeet (Neophema bourkii). *The normal has pink only on the abdomen, while the back is generally brown/grey.*

They are generally quiet, attractive, and fairly easy to keep and breed. They are susceptible to *paramyxovirus* infection and intestinal round-worms, so regular worming should be part of the management routine for these birds. Average lifespan for these little birds should be around fifteen years.

LARGER PARAKEETS

Like the first three groups, these are all long-tailed parrots, originating from the Old World (Eastern Hemisphere) and Australasia. In general they are best suited to outdoor aviary conditions, rather than being indoor caged birds. Many are noisy, and can be very destructive. Most are very colour-ful. They also require regular worming treatment. They could live for twenty-five to thirty years if well cared for.

Rosellas (*Platycercus* species)

This group is from Australasia, including medium-sized popular species of 25–35cm total length, and 100–120gm weight. They can be aggressive to each other, so should be kept in pairs, with double-wired flights or solid partitions, rather

than colonies. They have distinct coloured cheek patches, and scalloped feathering on the back and wings. Again, colour mutations have been bred in captivity. Common species include the Crimson rosella or Pennant *(Platycercus elegans)*, the Golden-mantled rosella *(P. flaveolus)* and the Mealy rosella *(P. adscitus)*.

ABOVE: *Golden-mantled rosellas* (Platycercus flaveolus) *showing the long tail, round head and small beak typical of this genus. White cheek patches are distinctive, while the scalloped yellow and black feathering of the back give these birds their common specific name. The two adult birds in the centre have brighter red feathering and less green than the two juveniles on either side.*

BELOW: *Golden-mantled rosella (GMR) mutation varieties. The central bird is the 'normal' colouring, other specimens show plumage variation.*

A further example of a mutation GMR, with lighter plumage colouring than the normal variety.

BELOW: *The very attractive Princess of Wales parakeet* (Polytelis alexandrae) *cock bird with its mix of pale pink, pale blue, and shades of green.*

The Barraband parakeet, or Superb parrot (Polytelis swainsonii) *cock bird, with its distinctive yellow face and red throat crescent. The hen of this species is mostly green, without the bright colouring of the male.*

Polytelis species

These birds are generally larger at 40–45cm than the Rosellas, and perhaps quieter and less aggressive. Several of these species are popular as aviary birds, including the Barraband (*Polytelis swainsonii*), the Princess of Wales parakeet (*P. alexandrae*) and the Rock pebbler (*P. anthopeplus*).

Red-rumped parakeets *(Psephotus haematonotus)*

These birds hail from Eastern Australia, and are larger than *Neophema* species at 27cm, but smaller than Rosellas. They are popular in aviculture, and have been used as foster-parents for other parakeet species. The adult male alone has the distinctive red-feathered rump: juveniles and females have green backs. They are probably not as long-lived as *Platycercus* and *Polytelis*, with average expectation being fifteen to twenty years.

Red-rumped parakeet (Psephotus haematonotus) *showing the distinctive red feathering on the lower back of the male. This bird is another captive-bred mutation, with pale olive-green plumage: the nominate race is darker green.*

Quaker or Monk Parakeet (Myiopsitta monachus) *showing the normal green and grey colouring of the normal species variety.*

Kakarikis (*Cyanoramphus* species)

These birds are of a similar size to Red-rumped parakeets, and are found in New Zealand. Two species are kept commonly in aviculture – the Red-fronted (*Cyanoramphus novaezelandiae*) and the Yellow-fronted (*C. auriceps*). The slatey-grey upper beak is a distinctive characteristic. They are comparatively quiet but attractive parrots, and will have a lifespan similar to the Red-rump.

Quaker (Monk) parakeets (*Myiopsitta monachus*)

These parrots are amongst the very few that build a nest of twigs and leaves rather than nesting in holes or tunnels. They nest communally, building large, untidy structures that will be added to every year. Hailing originally from Eastern Africa, they are now well-established not just in aviculture but also escapees have survived successfully in the wild in

Quaker or Monk parakeet (Myiopsitta monachus), *one of the species that has established feral populations in Europe. These birds build communal nests: such an untidy pile of twigs with two entrances may be seen in this palm tree.*

A blue mutation of the Quaker parakeet, with blue replacing the normal green.

Alexandrine parakeet (Psittacula eupatria), a larger cousin of the ring-necked parakeet. These species are sexually dimorphic, with visible differences between adult males and females. The male (cock) bird is on the right, with the row of pink and black feathers around its neck. Females (hens) and juveniles simply have light green feathers in this region. On closer inspection, there are also subtle differences in beak and head shape and size, detectable by experienced breeders, but this neck ring is very obvious.

parts of Europe and the USA. Slightly larger than red-rumps and kakarikis at 28–29cm and weighing about 100gm, the natural colour is green with a grey head, but in captivity blue, aqua and yellow mutations are found. They do have a raucous and repetitive call. Life expectancy in captivity would be fifteen to twenty years.

Ring-necked parakeets (*Psittacula* species)

Large, noisy, and destructive, these birds are widely distributed throughout Asia and parts of

Adult male Ring-necked parakeet (Psittacula krameri) showing the distinctive neck band of pink and black feathers.

Africa. They are popular in aviculture, but do need strongly-built aviaries. One should expect to replace wooden nest boxes and perches regularly, as they will be chewed readily! They have unusually long, tapering tails making up more than half of the total body length, and heavy, powerful beaks. Mature cock birds have distinctive head plumage-colouring that is absent in juveniles and females. They are not suited as indoor caged pets, as they are very active and need to fly. Their shrill screeching is loud and distinctive, and continues even when birds are in flight.

Common captive species include the attractive Plum-head parakeet (*Psittacula cyanocephala*), at just over 30cm the smallest of the group. The very common Ring-necked parakeet (*P. krameri*) is widespread across the Indian and African continents, popular in aviculture, and now large feral populations are well-established in Europe from avicultural escapees. The original species is predominantly green, but in captivity grey, blue, lutino and white mutations have been bred. Others include the Moustached Parakeet (*P. alexandri*) at 33cm; the Derbyan parakeet (*P. derbiana*) at 50cm; and the largest Alexandrine parakeet (*P. eupatria*) at 58cm. These larger birds could potentially live as long as forty years.

Sun conures (Aratinga solstitialis), *colourful but noisy members of this genus.*

striking, and the most frequently encountered, is the Sun conure *(Aratinga solstitialis)* at 30 cm length. Of similar size are the Jendaya conure *(A. jandaya)*, the Dusky-headed *(A. weddellii)*, the Brown-throated *(A. pertinax)* and the Nanday

Plum-headed parakeet (Psittacula cyanocephala) *showing his richly coloured head feathering, and long tail typical of this group of parakeets.*

Blue-crowned conure (Aratinga acuticaudata).

CONURES

The conures may be considered the South-American equivalents of the parakeets, having similar features of long tails of about the same length as the body, with streamlined shape and fast-flying behaviour. They generally have inquisitive, playful characters, and breed readily in captivity. There are two major groups, these being Aratinga and Pyrrhura.

Aratinga conures are larger and stockier than Pyrrhura species, and are both destructive and very noisy! They do have colourful personalities to match their vibrant plumage. Perhaps the most

Peachie, Peach-fronted conure (Aratinga aurea). *Note the mix of colours on the head of this attractive bird.*

(although this is a different genus – *Nandayus nenday*). Slightly larger at 35–40cm are the Blue-crowned conure *(A. acuticaudata)*, and several green-bodied species with varying amounts of red on the head such as the Mitred *(A. mitrata)*, Red-masked *(A. erythrogenys)* and the White-eyed *(A. leucophthalmus)*. Smaller at 25cm is the Peach-fronted *(A. aurea)*. Usual life expectancy for this group will be about thirty years.

Pyrrhura conures are somewhat quieter and smaller birds at about 25cm total length. They generally come in varying amounts of green,

A trio of Maroon-bellied conures (Pyrrhura frontalis).

Buzz, Patagonian conure (Cyanoliseus patagonus), a playful, multicoloured parrot.

brown, grey and maroon, although Painted conures *(Pyrrhura picta)* and Blue-throated *(P. cruentata)* are more colourful. The most common currently are the Maroon-bellied *(P. frontalis)* and the Green-cheeked *(P. molinae)*. These smaller birds will live for twenty to twenty-five years.

Two other genera in this group are represented commonly in aviculture. These are the Patagonian conures *(Cyanoliseus patagonus)* and the *Enicognathus species*. Patagonians are also known as burrowing parrots, as they nest in colonies in tunnels dug in sandy cliffs. They are large, with a total body length of 45cm. They are colourful and playful, but noisy! In common with other conures, they have long tapered tails, but their beaks are comparatively small in comparison

with their bodies. On the other hand the Slender-billed conure *(Enicognathus leptorhynchus)* and the Austral conure *(E. ferrugineus)* have elongated, slender upper beaks, used to dig for roots and tubers, and to winkle out seeds from cones. The Slender-billed is larger at 40cm, and is more frequently encountered in captivity than the smaller (30–35 cm) Austral. All of these species could live for twenty-five to thirty years.

Slender-billed conure (Enicognathus leptorhynchus), *showing the long upper beak (rostrum) using for digging up plant roots and bulbs. (Photo: Tony Pittman)*

Freddie, Green-cheeked conure (Pyrrhura molinae), *a smaller quieter bird than the* Aratinga *species.*

Peach-faced lovebirds (Agapornis roseicollis), *small, short-tailed parrots with green bodies and pale orange throats and faces.*

LOVEBIRDS (*AGAPORNIS* SPECIES)

Lovebirds are small parrots from Africa and Madagascar in a class of their own. They are stocky birds with short tails and strong beaks. They range from 15–20cm total length and 40–60gm bodyweight. In spite of their common name – derived from the strong pair bond and marked mutual preening in which many couples indulge – they can in fact be savagely aggressive to others of their kind that they do not get on with. They breed readily in captivity all year round, and they are noted for the appealing behaviour of tucking nest material under their wings to carry it to the nest. Birds will tear narrow strips of paper, or willow bark (their preferred material) for this purpose. The common variety is the Peach-faced lovebird (*Agapornis roseicollis*), another is the Black-masked (*A. personata*). Both these have been bred for generations in captivity, with numerous colour varieties. A third variety found in aviculture is the Fischer's (*A. fischeri*). Life expectancy would be around fifteen to twenty years on average.

ABOVE: *This picture also shows a blue mutation Black-masked lovebird* (Agapornis personata). *Its black head colouring makes the white eye-ring more pronounced.*

BELOW: *Green and yellow Black-masked lovebirds.*

LORIES AND LORIKEETS

This group includes a very large number of species of glossy, brightly coloured, vivacious, inquisitive birds from South-East Asia and Northern Australasia. They feed on nectar, pollen, fruits and flowers, and have slender, sharp-pointed beaks and brush-tipped tongues adapted to this diet. Currently numbers of breeding collections are falling as people find it very labour-intensive to provide the demanding diet of liquid nectar – which will ferment rapidly in warm weather and freeze in cold – as well as cope with the consequent

Duivenbode's lory (Chalcopsitta duivenbodei), *with iridescent brown and yellow plumage and a sharp hooked beak. These are very playful birds.*

The Red lory (Eos bornea). *Again notice the iridescent sheen to the plumage typical of this group, and the sharp-pointed upper beak.*

messy droppings. As a generalization, lories are larger birds with short rounded tails, while lorikeets are smaller birds with long slender tails. There are several genera and many species recognized, and considerable controversy over the identification and separation of sub-species. As these birds come from tropical islands, often each island will have its own variety that is subtly different from its neighbours, but whether these are true sub-species or simply local variations is continually debated.

Chalcopsitta is a genus of large birds of around 30cm length; the two most frequently encountered are *C. scintillate*, the Yellow-streaked, and *C. duivenbodei*, the Duivenbode's.

Trichoglossus is a large genus with many species and sub-species of multi-coloured birds, hence the group name of Rainbow lories for the many sub-species of *T. haematodus*. The generic name, of Greek origin, actually means 'hairy tongue', describing the distinctive papillae on the tongue tip.

Eos species include the Red lory (*E. bornea*), the Blue-streaked (*E. reticulate*) and the Violet-naped (*E. squamata*). The closely related Dusky lory (*Pseudeos fuscata*) is also popular.

Lorius garrulus, the Yellow-backed chattering lory, is another large, mostly red bird, with a patch of yellow feathers over the back. These larger species will all live for twenty-five to thirty years.

Dusky lories (Pseudeos fuscata) *are basically brown and red, but the iridescence and gradations of colour make it very attractive. These birds are eating sugar-coated sunflower kernels as treats, in a walk-through public aviary.*

Yellow-backed chattering lory (Lorius garrulus), *another colourful variety, showing the playful nature of these birds.*

The many smaller lorikeets include such enchanting species as the Goldie's, the Musschenbroek's, and the spectacular Stella's *(Charmosyna papou stellae)* with two long central feathers in its tail, like streamers, adding some 15cm to its length.

Some of these birds are kept as indoor caged pets, and they can be very entertaining characters, but their droppings are very liquid, sticky and ejected for a considerable distance.

SMALL PARROTS

There are several groups of small bodied, short-tailed parrots, popular and highly suitable as indoor family pets and with similar general characteristics, but coming from different parts of the world. All of these small parrots will have expected life-spans of around twenty-five to thirty years, but as always there are exceptions, with occasional upper limits of forty to fifty recorded.

Caiques originate from central South America, and are strong-willed but highly playful 'clowns' in their behaviour. They are entertaining pets, but can be very noisy and demanding, and require a strong-willed human to manage their dominating personality. They have mixed colours of green, white, yellow or orange, and in some cases black, with the colour being in well-demarcated areas on the body. The most common in captivity is the Black-headed caique *(Pionites melanocephala)* with White-bellied *(P. leucogaster)* also seen. Their eyes have rich orange-coloured irises.

Poicephalus parrots are of a similar size to the caiques, but come from Central and Southern Africa. They are squat bodied, with short, square-ended tails, and most are around 25cm in length. They may be considered as ideal household and family pet parrots. Most are neither excessively noisy nor destructive; when obtained young and hand-reared they have charming playful characters. Imported wild birds can be nervous and shy.

The most common is the Senegal parrot *(P. senegalus)*. These have green and orange bodies, with grey heads and striking yellow irises. All parrots have voluntary control of the muscles controlling their irises, but Senegals particularly will 'flash' their eyes by alternately dilating and constricting their pupils when excited, nervous or angry. Sexes have similar colouring, and although

Merlin, a Black-headed caique (Pionites melanocephala). *Note the feather colours in well-demarcated areas, and the rich orange colour of the iris.*

Paulie, a White-bellied caique (Pionites leocogaster). *There is a sub-species of this bird known as the Yellow-thighed caique.*

aviculturists claim that female birds have less extensive orange feathering on their bellies than the males, I have not found this to be supported by scientific sexing techniques. However, when several of these birds are grouped together for comparison, in 80 per cent of cases it is possible to pick out cock birds with wider heads and heavier beaks from the more delicate, finer-beaked hens.

Meyer's parrot (Poicephalus meyeri).

This applies also to the Meyer's Parrot *(P. meyeri)*, currently the second most popular of this group in captivity. Similar in character to the Senegal, although perhaps quieter, these are fundamentally grey and green (shading to blue in some individuals). There are distinctive yellow areas over the bend of the wing, and variable amounts of yellow feathering on the head. Their eyes have deep orangey-red irises.

Other species of the same size less commonly kept include the Brown-headed *(P. cryptoxanthus)*, the Red-bellied *(P. rufiventris)*, and Ruppell's parrot *(P. ruppellii)*. The Jardine's parrot *(P. gulielmi)* is a larger bird, reaching 28–30cm. It is predominantly green, being darker with marked black scalloping on the back and wings. There are variable amounts of orange colouring on the head, lower legs, and wings, with this orange increasing with maturity. The juvenile bird has no orange at all.

The largest of the group is the Cape (or Grey-headed) parrot *(P. robustus)*, reaching 32–33cm. They have large powerful beaks, and are primarily green, with dark grey tails and lighter grey heads. Scalloped edges to the feathers are obvious, and like the Jardine's the adult birds have variable amounts of orange on wing edges and lower legs. This species is unusual in that the adult hen bird is

There is slight geographical variation, with those birds coming from the Congo region generally being larger and lighter in colour than those from Cameroon and Ghana. General body colour is silvery grey, with marked scalloping to the feather edges, especially over the head and neck. The base of the back (rump) is a much paler silver colour, while the tail feathers in adult birds are bright red. Juvenile birds have darker-tipped tail feathers, replaced by the bright red at about one year old. It is a common problem for young birds to break or pull out their tail feathers during the first eighteen months of their lives.

The beak is all black, and there is a featherless area of white skin around the eyes. Rough handling of these birds will cause bruising of this facial skin very easily. The iris of the adult bird is yellow, while the juvenile bird has grey irises. The grey changes slowly to yellow at about one year old, and deepens in colour until full adulthood.

There is no marked morphological difference between the sexes, although experienced eyes may be able to pick out broad-skulled, heavy-beaked males from rounder-headed, slighter billed females with 80 per cent accuracy, if there is a large group of birds to choose from (*see* also Chapter 7).

Adult African grey cock bird. The beak is larger and heavier than most females, and the curve of the skull flows into the curve of the beak. Hen birds in general have a smaller beak, with a more pronounced 'stop' between forehead and beak base (see Chapter 7).

Quoted subtle differences of plumage – cock birds being darker than hens – are more geographical than sexual in this author's experience. The same applies to variation in shape of the bald white area around the eyes. The only reliable method of sex-determination is by scientific techniques of DNA-sampling or endoscopy (*see* page 129).

The popularity of these birds stems from their renowned ability as mimics. Whistles, squeaks, ring tones, doorbells and the like are mastered easily (*see* page 12). They will also pick up words and phrases, and do appear to have some comprehension of their meaning, as they tend to use them in the right context – for example 'Hello' when owners come into the room, 'Goodbye' as they leave, 'Goodnight' as lights are turned out. They will also associate names with objects or people – 'cat', 'dog', 'breakfast', 'Jack', 'Daddy', etc. Many individuals are notorious for swearing, but they mimic only what they hear repeatedly, so the owner is to blame, not the bird!

American animal psychologist Dr Irene Pepperberg carried out extensive behavioural testing on her grey parrot 'Alex' over a thirty-year period, demonstrating that he could recognize colours, shapes, textures, names of objects, and even concepts like 'bigger or smaller', 'same and different'. It is often quoted that parrots have the level of intelligence (as well as the attention span!) of a five-year-old human child.

Hand-reared young greys can be very tame, but as they mature they very often develop a preference for one person in the family. This may be sex-orientated, in that cock birds prefer women while hen birds relate to men. Adult birds can be very nervous, and will growl, flap, and throw themselves to the floor when approached.

These birds are more susceptible than most species to calcium-deficiency problems, resulting in soft bones, egg-related problems, or fits (seizures). They also will suffer from vitamin A deficiency and are extremely prone to feather plucking (*see* Chapter 8). Adult birds can be very selective feeders, choosing to pick out sunflower seeds and peanuts to the exclusion of all else. Younger birds that have been fed a more varied diet from an early age are easier in this respect but should not be allowed to lapse into bad habits (*see* Chapter 6).

Grey parrot showing a caseous mass removed from a sub-mandibular abscess, resulting from long-term dietary deficiency of vitamin A.

The Timneh grey parrot *(Psittacus erithacus timneh)* is a slightly smaller sub-species, having plumage of a darker grey, maroon tail feathers and a horn-coloured upper beak. They are perhaps calmer and quieter than the nominate species, but with the same mimicking ability. They are less readily available than silver greys, but are cheaper, and make excellent pets with potentially fewer behavioural problems.

Gizmo, Timneh grey parrot (Psittacus erithacus timneh), *showing the patch of horn-colour on the beak, the dark maroon tail feathers, and the smaller, darker body compared with the standard silver grey parrot.*

Life expectancy for both standard silver greys and timnehs as pet birds is usually thirty-five to forty years. Aviary breeding birds usually are worn out a little sooner.

Amazon Parrots

Amazon parrots include a large group of popular species, named for their natural habitat of the Amazon basin in South America. At least, the majority come from this region: some of the rarer species are found on individual Caribbean islands. Some of these endangered species – like the St Vincent *(Amazona guildingii)* – are large (40cm) heavy birds, and highly coloured. Most of the more common species in captivity are primarily green, with varying amounts of yellow, blue and red or orange. These types are either 30cm long and weighing around 400gm, with a lifespan similar to the greys of thirty-five to forty years; or there is a smaller group of 25–28cm.

Because of their origins in tropical rainforest, these parrots enjoy and even need both a high percentage of fruit and vegetable in their diet, and regular soaking with water. Outdoor aviary birds or those living wild in their wet forests have rich plumage colours with a healthy sheen. They will spread their wings, hang upside down, and thoroughly enjoy a heavy downpour. Indoor parrots that are not sprayed regularly, by comparison are often dull and dowdy. Amazon plumage has a distinctive sweet smell, and they are less dusty than grey parrots. Indoor specimens have a tendency to obesity because of their sedentary lifestyle, especially if fed a dry-seed mix (*see* Chapter 6).

The common captive species are generally interesting, playful characters, and less inclined to become 'one-person' birds. Their big disadvantage is their natural vocalization at dawn and dusk. They will chatter and squawk throughout the day, and will learn to mimic human speech and other sounds. They appear to be quite 'musical' in their normal vocal range, and will mimic opera and other human music well. However, when they really let rip at daybreak and early evening, the volume produced is incredible, although it is perhaps marginally more tolerable than the

Yellow-naped Amazons (Amazona auropalliata) *defending their nest box. Note the constricted pupils of the bird on the right, illustrating a threat display. (Photo: Jan Hooimeijer DVM)*

Adult Orange-winged Amazon showing the generally green body colouring of most of the common Amazon species, with yellow chin and lores, and a lilac-blue crown.

harsh screeching of the cockatoos or the raucous squawks of the macaws!

Breeding pairs can be very territorial and protective of their nest sites, and will expend a lot of energy facing up to neighbouring pairs. Indoor cock birds that become bonded to human carers may be dangerously aggressive to perceived 'rivals' or 'intruders'. These birds probably more than any other will use the voluntary control over their iris muscles to 'flash' their eyes in an emotional response. Juvenile birds have brown irises, which become more orange as the birds mature.

There are several species available and considerable controversy over various sub-species and geographical races. There is wide colour variation within each species that may simply reflect geographical origin, but this fact has led to disagreement amongst taxonomists as to whether one type may be a sub-species or even a separate species, or simply an intra-species variety. Improved techniques of chromosomal karyotyping (DNA analysis) will ultimately settle such arguments. The situation is complicated by the ability of these birds to hybridize across species.

The most frequently encountered species in captivity are the Orange-winged Amazon *(Amazona amazonica)*, the Blue-fronted *(A. aestiva)*, and the several varieties of Yellow-headed *(A. ochrocephala)*. As with African grey parrots and some *Poicephalus* species, experienced observers may be able to identify cock birds with broad flat heads and heavy beaks in comparison with the rounder head and smaller beak of the female. In general, however, there is no obvious sexual dimorphism. Orange-winged Amazons have green bodies and wings, with orange colouring under the tail and on

Wing feathers of Amazona aestiva *showing the red colouring among the green, blue and black. Note the new feather at P7, shorter and richer in colour than the rest.*

Fledgling Blue-fronted Amazon (Amazona aestiva), *showing growing feathers with grey down, and the dark brown iris typical of the young bird.*

the mid-flight feathers of the wings. The cheeks and forehead are a primrose-yellow, although the area of yellow above the beak varies considerably in extent. Between the two yellow areas, and extending around the eyes, are sky-blue feathers. Their beaks are a mixture of grey, black and horn colours. Blue-fronted Amazons have very similar

Young Blue-fronted Amazon helping itself to some spoon-feeding!

colouring, but with red feathers in the wings, black beaks, and with the blue feathering directly above the beak on the forehead. In this case the blue is more turquoise than sky-blue. Yellow feathers are found on the cheeks and throat, and on top of the head behind the blue. The extent of this yellow is extremely variable, as may be seen from the various illustrations.

Yellow-headed Amazons have many variations, and it is perhaps this group that provokes most discussion about various sub-species and races. Broadly speaking, the varieties most common seen in captivity are the following: Yellow-fronted or Yellow-crowned (*A. ochrocephala ochrocephala*), green bodied with red in the wings and an area of yellow feathering on the forehead only; the beak is dark. Panama Amazon (*A. o. panamensis*), similar to the above, but with a pale coloured beak. Yellow-naped Amazon (*A. o. auropalliata*), no (or minimal) yellow on the forehead, but instead a crescent of yellow at the back of the neck. Yellow-headed and Double Yellow-headed (*A. o. oratrix* and *A. o. tresmariae*) both have yellow feathers on the entire head and neck; in *tresmariae* it extends down onto the chest.

The Lilac-crowned Amazon (*A. finschii*) is encountered less commonly, and has no yellow feathering at all, but a green body with red on

Lilac-crowned Amazon (Amazona finschii), *with the green scalloped body feathers, pale beak, and reddish crown. This is a young bird: the adult shading tends to be paler and more lilac than red.*

Yellow-fronted (Crowned) Amazon (Amazona ochrocephala) *with a band of yellow feathers on the forehead, but no blue.*

the wings and lores (area above the nostrils), green cheeks, and lilac feathering on the crown of the head and nape of the neck; the beak is pale. The Primrose-cheeked or Red-lored Amazon *(A. autumnalis)* is a pretty bird with a green body and red wing flashes. The head is coloured with red at the lores, yellow on the cheeks, and lilac-blue on the crown.

The Mealy Amazon *(A. farinosa)* is generally larger than all of the above, being 38–40cm long. For their size they are gentle, tolerant birds, but when they choose to vocalize they have the loudest voices of the group! They are not as commonly encountered, partly because their colouring is less interesting, being mostly green with a small amount of yellow on the head and blue shading of the nape and back; but also because they are difficult to breed in captivity. There appears to be a disproportionate ratio of hens to cocks around, with just one hen available to every nine or ten cocks.

Smaller Amazon parrots are encountered, although less frequently. They are around 25cm in length and generally green with variable head colouring. Most are specialist breeders' birds rather than pet specimens, with the exception of the White-fronted Amazon *(A. albifrons)*. This parrot is unusual in this genus, in that it is visibly sexually dimorphic: all birds have green bodies with white

Cock Eclectus parrot Chocky showing prolonged and severe feather mutilation, common in this species.

but purist collectors prefer to keep the various sub-species intact to breed with others of their own kind.

Most of the time these birds appear to sit quietly and watch the world go by, seemingly 'taking it all in'. However, when they do suddenly let rip their calls can be loud and raucous. The females are dominant over the males, and like to spend most of their time in the nest box, if established as a breeding pair. Many pet individuals (especially cock birds) are susceptible to serious and persistent feather mutilation.

Their digestive tracts are well adapted to a high-fibre fruit and vegetable diet, and these items should be essential feeding for these birds. Like African grey parrots, they appear particularly susceptible to calcium deficiency diseases, and to a lesser extent hypovitaminosis-A. Average lifespan should be thirty-five to forty years, but many do not achieve this because of ignorance of their nutritional needs.

lores, blue crown, and red around the eyes, but only adult males have red feathers on the leading edge of the wing. The beak is yellow.

Eclectus Parrots are also unusual in being markedly sexually dimorphic. Cock birds are bright luminous green, with varying patches of red and occasionally blue. His upper beak is orange-yellow. Hens are primarily deep red, with some races having blue, mauve, or yellow areas, and a black beak. The nominate species is *Eclectus roratus*, but originating from the many islands of the Australasian Pacific, there are several sub-species and geographical races. They will interbreed freely,

Vasa parrots are rarely encountered as pets, but several aviculturists keep them in breeding collections. They are unusual birds in many ways, and are considered to be comparatively primitive parrot species. They originate from Madagascar and neighbouring islands off the east coast of Africa. They have an all-over charcoal grey plumage, with white periorbital skin and pale beaks. Some feathers may show as brown or blue-green depending on the angle of the light, but any individuals that show white feathering should be viewed with suspicion.

Lesser vasa parrots (Coracopsis nigra) *with white feathers in the plumage associated with infection with the virus causing psittacine beak and feather disease (PBFD). This is a distinctive feature in this species, and makes the presence of the infection readily identifiable.*

This is generally an indication of infection with psittacine beak and feather disease (PBFD) virus, to which these birds are highly susceptible. There are two species – the Greater vasa *(Coracopsis vasa)* and the Lesser vasa *(Coracopsis nigra)*. Both have slimmer bodies and longer tails than the Amazons, greys and Eclectus. The Greater has an over-all length of 50cm, the Lesser is 35cm.

Further interesting facts about these unique birds relate to their breeding. The Lesser has the shortest incubation period of any parrot, at just fourteen days. Both sexes of both species have large pink protuberances from their vents (cloaca) in the breeding season, which on many occasions have been confused with an abnormal cloacal pro-lapse. Finally, hen birds lose their head feathers in the breeding season, and the skin of the head becomes quite yellow. This effect is more marked in the Greater species.

MACAWS

These birds are the classic 'pirate's parrot': the long-tailed, colourful, characterful birds of child-hood comics, cartoons, pantomimes and feature films. Hailing from the tropical rainforests of Central and South America, these are loud, socia-ble birds. In the wild they forage for nuts, seeds, berries and fruit. In captivity they are active and entertaining. They will learn to talk, play actively with toys, and perform simple tasks. However, they can be noisy and destructive, and require plenty of space.

Like Amazons, they may be divided broadly into two groups – the larger macaws and the dwarf macaws.

Large Macaws

The magnificent Hyacinthine macaw *(Anodo-rhynchus hyacinthinus)* is the largest of the common captive species, being 100cm long including the tail, and weighing over 1.5kg. Its plumage is an iridescent rich violet blue, with distinctive areas of naked, bright yellow skin under the lower mandi-ble and around the eyes. The huge beak is black. Its favourite foods in the wild are palm nuts, and

Green-winged macaw (Ara chloroptera) – *the classic large parrot beloved of cartoons and films. Note the long tail and large, powerful beak.*

like all large macaws in captivity should have nuts in shell provided in their diet. The huge, powerful beak will make short work of breaking open the thickest of shells.

They are slow breeders, and habitat destruction in the wild has endangered free-living populations. In the USA, captive numbers are considerable, and many are found as pets, but in the UK and Western Europe the smaller numbers that do exist are generally for attempted breeding rather than

The magnificent Hyacinthine macaw (Anodorhynchus hyacinthinus), *with violet-blue feathers, bright yellow chin and eye ring, and large black beak. (Photo: Tony Pittman)*

The Blue-throated or Caninde macaw (Ara glaucogularis) *showing the blue feathering on throat and face and no green forehead.*

pet birds. Their size, colour, and scarcity make them very expensive birds. Those that are lucky enough to keep these giants find them usually to be very gentle, tolerant parrots.

The remaining common captive large macaws are all from the genus *Ara*. These are distinguished by bright colours, large heavy beaks, and a bald area of white facial skin. Like the grey parrot, this skin may flush pink when the bird is excited or angry, and certainly will bruise easily if the bird is roughly handled. All these macaws (if healthy) have a distinctive – though not unpleasant – smell about their plumage. Life expectancy should be fifty to sixty years. Reports of them reaching a hundred years are generally exaggerated, but potentially possible.

The largest of the group is the Green-winged macaw *(Ara chloroptera)* at 90cm, and like the Hyacinthine may be considered a 'gentle giant'. Their temperament in captivity is generally good if well-treated and respected, with plenty of space, good feeding, and toys to play with and wood to chew. Body feathers are a deep red, with lines of small red feathers across the white facial skin. Tail feathers are blue and red, while the rump is pale blue. The wings have red shoulder areas, then a band of dark green coverts, while the flight feathers are dark blue. The lower beak is black, while the upper part is black and cream.

Probably the most common of the captive species is the Blue and yellow (Blue and gold) macaw *(Ara ararauna)*. Slightly smaller than the green-winged at 85–90cm, this bird has bright blue plumage on the back, wings, neck and outer tail, with a rich yellow chest and abdomen, and

darker yellow shading on the underside of the tail feathers. Several pictures are featured in this book, reflecting their popularity. The brow of the head shades from blue to green, and there is a crescent of black feathers under the lower jaw. These black feathers extend in lines across the face. The endangered Blue-throated or Caninde macaw *(Ara glaucogularis)* is similar in colouring except that it lacks the green on the forehead, while the throat and facial lines are blue rather than black. The beak is all black in both these species.

Green-winged macaw's head showing distinctive lines of red feathers that are almost as unique as human fingerprints, with every bird having a slightly different pattern. Note also the yellow iris, denoting an adult bird, and the heavy, horn-coloured upper beak.

Blue and yellow macaw in close-up, showing the various feather colours around the face, the facial lines of green-black feathers, the grey-yellow iris denoting a young adult, the large black beak, the nostril in the fleshy cere, and the white facial skin.

Blue and yellow macaw (Ara ararauna), *probably the most common of the large macaws in captivity. Note again the long tail, equal in length to the body and head combined.*

The Scarlet macaw *(Ara macao)* is marginally smaller, rarely exceeding 85cm. General colouring is similar to the green-winged, except the red is lighter, more orangey, and the green wing coverts of the latter species are replaced by a broad band of yellow feathers in the scarlet. There are no facial lines in this species. The beak is similarly coloured to the green-winged, having a black mandible and a black and cream rostrum. Although colourful and popular, these macaws can be more aggressive and temperamental than their larger cousins, and will require careful management for this reason. Both the scarlet and the blue-and-yellow macaws breed well in captivity.

Buffon's macaw *(Ara ambigua)* and the Military macaw *(Ara militaris)* are found less commonly, and mostly in breeding collections, rather than as pet birds. Both are primarily green, with red across the forehead and some blue in the tail. The Buffon's is larger at 85cm and is a comparatively quiet, inactive bird. The military, at 70cm, is more agile and active, as well as being noisier. The facial skin of these two species flushes red more readily than any of the other large macaws.

Hybrid Macaws

Like several of the Amazon parrot species, these large *Ara* species inhabit similar areas, and being in the same genus can interbreed and hybridize. In some countries, this practice has been encouraged in captivity, to the point where specific crosses have been given names. Thus there is the Catalina resulting from a cross between a scarlet and a blue-and-yellow; the Harlequin from a blue-and-yellow x green-winged; and the Ruby from a scarlet x green-winged. It can go beyond that – further cross-breeding for example of a Catalina with a scarlet produces a Camelot!

Dwarf Macaws

These birds are dwarf only in comparison to their larger cousins, but some are still sizeable birds. With the exception of the Hahns' Macaw, few are kept as pets. Most specimens in captivity are in breeding collections, and make suitable subjects for those with limited space wishing to keep and breed macaws. They can still be noisy and destructive, so strong aviary construction with suitable gauge mesh is necessary (*see* Chapter 4).

They are all predominantly green birds, with the similar long tails and featherless cheeks of their larger cousins. The largest is the 50cm Red-bellied macaw *(Ara manilata)*, with blue-green plumage, apart from a patch of red on the abdomen, and markedly yellow facial skin in adult birds. These have been imported in large numbers in the past, but have proved to be nervous, difficult to keep, and prone to obesity. Slightly smaller at 46cm is the Chestnut-fronted or Severe macaw *(Ara severa)*, with green body, green and blue wings with red flashes, a red/brown tail, and deep brown colouring of the lores and chin. Like its larger cousins the green-winged and blue-and-yellow, this species has lines of feathers across its white facial skin. Both these macaws have black beaks.

Yellow-collared (or yellow-naped) macaws *(Ara auricollis)* reaching about 40cm have similar body, wing and tail colouring to the chestnut-fronted, but without the red wing flashes. Their cheeks are pale yellow, with no feathering, and there is a band of yellow feathers around the nape of the neck. Illiger's and Blue-headed macaws are similar in size, but far less common.

The Hahn's macaw is a sub-species of *Ara nobilis,* and at just 30cm is the smallest of the group. It is commonly encountered as a pet, and is lively, playful and inquisitive. It can be spiteful if not properly managed, and has a shrill, repetitive call. It is a green bird, with yellow-green wing and tail feathers, red shoulder flashes, and bluish head. The beak is dark grey or black, and the cheeks are white.

Hahn's macaw (Ara nobilis) *with its green feathering, naked cheeks, and orange-brown irises. Its dark beak is flaky, indicating possible nutritional imbalance, while the shoulder area of the wing is plucked – a very common problem in this species.*

COCKATOOS

The final group of parrots to be considered here originates from Australasia and South-East Asia. They include species popular in aviculture and so widespread in their native habitats as to be considered pest species, through to endangered and uncommon types.

These parrots are distinguished by the possession of erectile crest feathers on their heads, displayed under voluntary control in response to emotions such as fear, excitement, aggression, or territorial display. Unlike all other parrot species, they have no blue or green colouration in their plumage. Broadly, there are two groups – the black cockatoos and the white cockatoos – with the pink and grey Roseate cockatoo being the exception.

Black Cockatoos

The black cockatoos will not be discussed in detail here: those in captivity are for specialist collectors rather than hobbyist aviculturists, and most are found in comparatively small numbers in the wild. The genus *Calyptorhynchus* includes the red-tailed black, the white-tailed black, the yellow-tailed black, and the glossy cockatoo. These have short crest feathers; long, rounded tails; and stocky powerful beaks. There is sexual dimorphism, with males having the colours in the tail that give each species its name, while females tend to be duller, and with spotting or barring of the body feathers. Body size is 60–65cm.

The black Palm cockatoo (*Probosciger aterrimus*) is a striking bird owing to its prominent crest, huge macaw-like beak and naked cheek patches that flush red with emotion. The feet are comparatively small, and the tongue is distinctively bi-coloured, being pink/red like the cheeks for most of its length, but with a black tip. The beak is black in adult birds, but in common with many parrots is a lighter grey or horn colour in juveniles. Total body length is 60–65cm, and these birds potentially could live to fifty to sixty years. They are found in captivity with specialist collectors, but can prove difficult to maintain and breed. They reproduce only slowly, laying just a single egg and rarely breeding every season. They favour a deep vertical nest in a hollow tree trunk.

The Gang-gang cockatoo (*Callocephalon fimbriatum*) is a smaller bird at some 35cm, and is distinctively sexually dimorphic: the cock bird has red crest feathers while the hen's are grey. This colour distinction is visible as soon as chicks fledge in the nest, making this and the Eclectus the only parrot species that can be reliably visibly sexed at this early age. The short curly crest is not as mobile as those of the other cockatoos. The few individuals that are kept captive appear to be highly susceptible to self-mutilation of their feathers.

The Roseate or Galah cockatoo (*Eolophus roseicapillus*) is a distinctive pink and grey bird, with a short but expressive crest. Like most of the white cockatoos, there is visible sexual dimorphism in adult individuals, in that hen birds have

Roseate (Galah) cockatoo (Eolophus roseicapillus), *a pest species in its native Australia, but an expensive pet in the western world. The body feathers are pink and grey, while the crest is a paler pink. The beak is small and pale in colour.*

reddish-brown irises while cock birds' irises are dark brown/black. The front of the body, face and head are pink, while the back, wings and tail are grey. The crest feathers on the crown of the head are paler than the remaining pink plumage. The depth of colour varies with individuals: once again this may reflect geographical areas of origin. They breed successfully in captivity, and white and cinnamon mutations have been produced.

The small area of naked skin around the eyes (periophthalmic ring) can become quite nodular in appearance and deep pink in colour in adult breeding birds, especially males. The beak is comparatively small, and is grey or horn-coloured. These birds are primarily ground feeders, taking seeds, grains, roots, young shoots and small insects. This behaviour and their large numbers across most of Australia make them unpopular with farmers, since they devastate growing crops as well as stored grain. In captivity, they have a marked tendency to obesity and the development of fatty tumours (lipomata) if they are fed on a large-seed diet high in sunflower.

Compared with their white cousins, they are comparatively quiet birds, their calls being a warbling chatter, although they can produce higher-volume shrieks if they so choose. They are playful, inquisitive characters, with a potential lifespan of thirty to fifty years. In captivity, mutation colours have been bred, including the cinnamon, but these are without exception smaller and weaker than their natural original strains.

White Cockatoos

The white cockatoos include several species common in captivity, both in breeding collections and as pet birds.

However, these are demanding birds, and probably more than other parrot types they are likely to end their days in parrot sanctuaries and rescue centres. They have been bred successfully and prolifically in the last forty years, and the tendency for hand-reared young cockatoos to behave as appealing cuddly-tame babies has entranced many an unwary buyer in to purchasing one of these birds without fully appreciating what they are taking on. Almost without exception, these humanized babies grow to sexual maturity with serious issues relating to their own ability to identify with other birds, having been brought up as 'people'. This, coupled with humans misinterpreting their needs and behaviour patterns, leads to a pet that screams, becomes aggressive and unpredictable, or severely feather-plucks and self-mutilates. Such birds are often passed on to new homes when the owner cannot cope, with this pattern repeated until the bird ends up in a rescue centre.

Aviary collections of breeding cockatoos, on the other hand, are generally trouble-free, as long as neighbours accept their noise. They happily get on with their lives as parrots, without the psychological hang-ups of their indoor cousins. They do need spacious and strongly constructed aviaries. All these birds are destructive chewers, and need ample supplies of fresh wooden toys, perches and nest-boxes. All these birds produce large quantities of white feather dust from their plumage; at the least this will upset the house-proud owner, and at worst can result in allergic reactions or lung damage in sensitive human individuals.

Sulphur-crested cockatoos include a number of familiar species. The Lesser sulphur-crested (*Cacatua sulphurea*) has two common varieties: the standard 30–35cm white bird with lemon-yellow cheeks and crest feathers, and dark grey legs and

A pair of Citron-crested cockatoos (Cacatua sulphurea citrinocristata). *Bingo on the left is the male, with dark eyes; Maxi the hen has red-brown eyes. She also is overweight, showing sagging fatty areas above her thighs. Both birds are chronic feather-pluckers – a common problem in captive white cockatoos.*

Medium Sulphur-crested cockatoo Saxo, a bright white bird with a lemon-yellow crest. Notice the fluffed feathers of the cheek spread across the beak, typical of these birds when relaxed.

Goffin's cockatoo (Cacatua goffini) with its small crest and beak, and pale pink areas around the head.

beak; or the Citron-crested *(C sulphurea citrinoc-ristata)* where the cheeks and crest feathers are closer to orange. Another sub-species of Cacatua sulphurea, being slightly larger at 35–40cm, is known as the Medium sulphur-crested, but is otherwise similar to the nominate species.

The Greater sulphur-crested cockatoo *(Cacatua galerita)* is a much larger bird at 50cm, although with a comparatively smaller beak, and otherwise similar in colouring. The yellow crest feathers have more of a forward curve than Lessers. The sub-species *C galerita triton* has a blue periophthalmic ring.

The smaller Goffin's cockatoo *(Cacatua goffini)* at 30–32cm has gained in popularity in recent years, being perhaps quieter than the other whites. It has a small rounded crest, and a generally white body, with salmon pink around the face plus pale yellow under the tail. The similar sized

Red-vented cockatoo *(Cacatua haematuropygia)* and the Ducorps *(C ducorpsii)* are seen occasionally in specialist breeding collection but rarely as pet birds.

The Bare-eyed cockatoo or Little corella *(Cacatua sanguinea)* has a large naked blue-grey periophthalmic area, but otherwise is similar in appearance to the Goffin's. It is another wide-spread pest species in its native Australia. The Long-billed or Slender-billed corella *(Cacatua ten-uirostris)* is larger at 38cm and less stocky. It also

Bare-eyed cockatoo (Cacatua sanguinea) *is similar in appearance to the Goffin's cockatoo, with a short crest, but with a naked periophthalmic ring of pale blue skin.*

Long-billed corella (Cacatua tenuirostris) has deep salmon-pink patches around the face and throat. The bird is pictured here with two Sulphur-crested cockatoos and the larger Moluccan cockatoo.

Dougal, Umbrella cockatoo (Cacatua alba) displaying his impressive large white crest feathers. The black beak is covered with white dust, produced in quantity by all white cockatoos, and indicative of healthy plumage. His breast, however, is chronically plucked.

has a blue periophthalmic ring, and deep salmon-pink patches on the neck and face.

The Umbrella or white cockatoo *(Cacatua alba)* is so named for its all-white plumage (except for a pale yellow under the wings and its very large crest, with round-ended feathers, in contrast to the tapered crest feathers of the sulphur-crests). It reaches a total length of around 45cm, and is bred commonly in captivity, being one of those examples of types sold as cuddly baby pets, but becoming noisy, destructive, and demanding with maturity. They are very susceptible to plucking problems.

The large (50–55cm) Moluccan or Salmon-crested cockatoo *(Cacatua moluccensis)* is a striking bird, with an over-all pale pink suffusion to its body feathers, pale yellow under the tail, and deep salmon pink, round-ended crest feathers. There is a pale periophthalmic ring, and the legs and beak – like most of this group – are dark grey. These parrots are popular in captivity, and are bred frequently, flooding the pet market with demanding babies. They have a loud quavering cry, and a very loud shrill screech. They are active chewers, and require plenty of wood to keep them occupied. Feather-plucking and self-mutilation are common in this species if they do not receive the care, space, attention, and occupation that they need and deserve.

Finally in this group, although it is hardly a white cockatoo, is the spectacular Major Mitchell's or Leadbeater's cockatoo *(Cacatua leadbeateri)*. The wings and tail are mostly white on their outer surface, but their undersides, plus the body and head, are pale pink, with a band of deeper pink above the beak. The striking crest feathers curve forwards when raised, and are scarlet-red, tipped with white, and with a central band of yellow. The beak is small and pale grey. Its body size is similar to the Lesser-sulphurs and Citrons at 35cm.

All these cockatoos can live for forty to seventy years, but behavioural problems leading to frequent change of ownership, poor diet and obesity, and general misunderstanding of their needs in captivity will often shorten this potential span.

There are some other parrots pictured throughout the book, which are described in the captions, but these are not included here since they are not considered to be popular or common species.

Moluccan cockatoo (Cacatua moluccensis) *with its black beak and pale pink plumage, with a darker, salmon-pink crest.*

Major Mitchell's or Leadbeater's cockatoo (Cacatua leadbeateri) *with its dramatic tri-coloured, forward-curving crest feathers. Body plumage is white and pink, and the beak is small and pale coloured. Note the short, rounded, fleshy tongue typical of all parrots except lories.*

CHAPTER 4

Housing Inside or Out?

The preceding chapters may seem to be full of negative comments about the disadvantages and pitfalls of parrot-keeping. Good! This is a serious commitment, not to be taken lightly, and you need to be very sure about what you are taking on. However, if you are reading this book you are obviously serious about your interest. The difficulty lies in reaching and educating those people who do not read books such as this before embarking on a potentially stressful, committed, long-term relationship. The plus side is that there is a lot of joy and pleasure to be had from parrot keeping.

As outlined in Chapter 2, the selection of your birds will be influenced by the major choice between keeping one or more pet parrots indoors, or housing a larger number of birds in outdoor aviaries, and maybe breeding from them.

AVIARY FOR OUTDOOR BIRDS

There is no doubt that parrots benefit significantly from living outdoors. Fresh air, natural sunlight, rainfall, and enriched environment, with room to spread their wings and fly, all result generally in fitter, healthier birds. We rarely see plucked parrots living in outdoor aviaries, other than those that were already chronically plucked before ending up in a sanctuary.

However, there are also disadvantages. The ever-present and increasing risk of theft makes outdoor birds more vulnerable. Predator hazards such as birds of prey, cats, rats and stoats may kill or maim aviary inmates, or raid their nests. Native birds such as pigeons and starlings, or small mammals such as rats or mice, may spread infectious diseases via their droppings. Environmental

hazards such as bonfire or barbecue smoke, traffic fumes, or even insecticides sprayed nearby, may cause disease or death.

Finally there is the worry of noisy birds, at best irritating your neighbours, and at worst leading to ugly disputes, litigation, and the possibility of losing your birds. Involve your neighbours at the outset and discuss your plans. Tailor the species kept according to the proximity of your neighbours and the potential noise-carrying capacity of various parrots. Think of screening with walls, fences, or dense shrubs and trees.

Naturally, parrots are at their noisiest as they call to each other at dawn and dusk, or during the breeding season. This may be controlled up to a point by keeping the birds shut into a sound-proofed house until a reasonable hour in the morning, and putting them away again in the early evening. Brick or block-built buildings with

Large outdoor aviary at a public bird garden, with Green-winged and Scarlet macaws. Construction is of brick and wood, with heavy-gauge wire mesh and large branches for perching.

CASE STUDY: ANYTHING WRONG?

Scarlet macaws (Ara macao). *Adult (left) and juvenile (right)*.

Jack, a scarlet macaw *(Ara macao)* and his owner Paul had a regular morning routine whereby as Paul changed the food and water bowls at the front of the aviary, the bird would approach from his resting place at the far end of his roosting perch and say 'Hello'. A simple greeting, but one that had become a regular ritual between owner and bird. Every bird-keeper will have a similar tale of such behavioural idiosyncrasies: it is part of the fascination of bird keeping, but it is also an important aspect of the bird's normal healthy routine.

One morning Paul was doing his round as usual, but Jack stayed quietly on his perch at the back of the flight. He looked fine: bright-eyed, alert, and with normal droppings under the perch, but he would not come forward with his usual greeting.

Paul continued round the rest of his extensive collection, but when he had finished feeding and watering he had the presence of mind to come back to Jack's flight. (Many owners would have shrugged their shoulders, thinking 'He looks fine', and left it until the following morning.) Now, under the bird's perch, was a dropping filled with bright red blood!

Alarmed at what he saw, Paul immediately telephoned me for assistance. After examining the by-now subdued and quiet bird, and a few simple diagnostic tests, we ascertained that Jack was suffering from zinc poisoning. Heavy metals such as zinc and lead are common causes of poisoning in birds, and the passing of fresh blood is a distinctive sign in such cases.

It turned out that Paul had recently repaired some of Jack's destructive 'modifications' to his flight with a new roll of galvanized wire mesh. Jack had happily been picking away at the globules of zinc that collected at the wire crossover points, and eventually ingested sufficient to make him unwell.

A hard lesson learned, but thanks to the owner's awareness of his bird's normal behaviour, prompt diagnosis and appropriate treatment, Jack made a rapid and full recovery.

Droppings filled with bright fresh blood. This indicates bleeding from the lower bowel, and is most frequently associated with heavy metal poisoning – lead or zinc.

Layout

If the aviary is used as year-round accommodation for your birds, security and weather-proofing are extra important. Temperate climates require protection from frost, rain and snow; other areas may require provision for hurricanes or typhoons, or flooding. Alternatively, the flights may be used simply for daily exercise and fresh air, or just for 'fair-weather' living.

Either way, the ideal arrangement is a 'three-thirds' setup. One third of the length of the aviary is secure, sheltered housing; one third is wired flight that is covered with a roof; while the final third is wired flight open to the elements. This gives the birds warmth, shelter, security and a place to roost, feed or breed in safety in the 'shed' area. Your birds may be shut in this section by closing the access to the flight, if you wish to reduce the noise nuisance to neighbours; to carry out cleaning or maintenance in the flight; or to facilitate capture, handling and treatment of the birds.

While in the outside flight, they may choose to shelter under the roofed area from hot sun or heavy rain and snow, but they will enjoy the open area in fine weather or light showers.

Positioning of the aviary is important. If it is visible from the house, you will be able to see and enjoy your birds more, as well as this being a more secure situation. CCTV or an alarm system should be a major consideration. Screening from neighbours with a high hedge or fence is sensible, but you should also allow room for expansion. It is inevitable that as you become gripped by the hobby of parrot-keeping, you will want to take on more birds, so choose an area where it will be

An ideal aviary with enclosed section, covered flight and open flight.

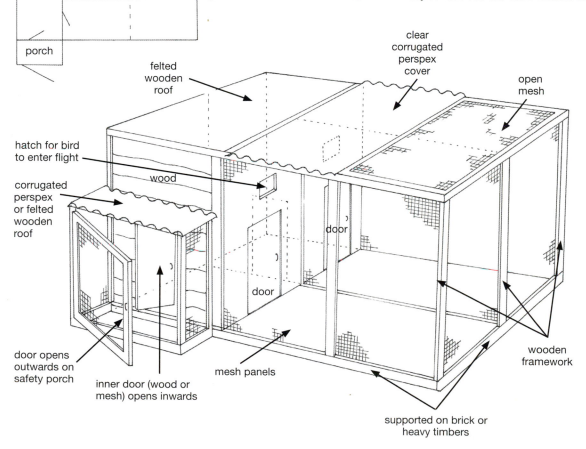

General view of a large garden aviary built of treated wood attached to partially buried sleepers, with double-wired mesh panels. There is a service corridor along the back (not shown), with three wooden 'houses' opening out into the covered flights at the front of the picture. The roofing here is corrugated perspex sheet. At the far end is the larger communal flight, with no roofing, so the birds have full access to sunlight and rain showers.

Prefabricated metal aviary showing a 'safety porch' at the front end. The keeper can enter this section and close the door behind them, before entering the aviary proper, thus preventing the escape of birds from the aviary.

Safety porch on a wood and metal flight, showing the same principle of secure entry to the aviary by shutting the outer door before opening the inner, and vice versa. However, operation would be simpler if the outer door had been hinged to open outwards.

easier to add-on new flights, rather than having to tear down your aviaries and start again!

A safety porch is a must. Too many times I have seen or heard of birds flying out past their owners as they open the only access door to the flight. Low-level doors that necessitate the owner crouching down to enter the aviary will reduce the risk – since birds are less likely to fly down so low to escape – but will not altogether negate it. A bank of aviaries may have an access corridor along the back, allowing individual approach to each flight from within the corridor. The main door should be closed securely on entering, and then any bird that escapes from its flight will be contained within the corridor. This system also makes access to food and water and cleaning of each flight far easier than the alternative arrangement of a safety porch on the end of the bank of aviaries, with each flight then entered in turn from its predecessor. This is more awkward, and involves more disturbance to the birds, as well as the necessity to carry several bowls and buckets through each flight.

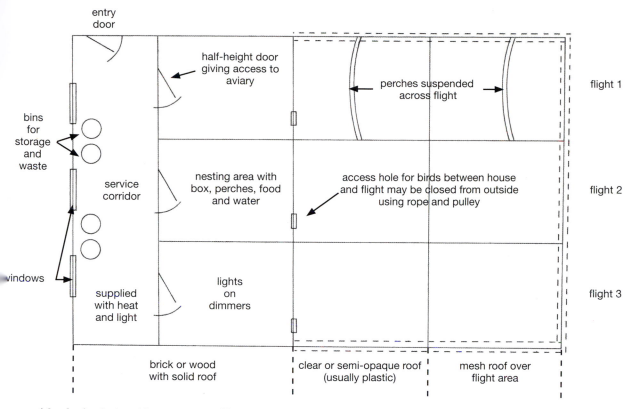

entry
door

half-height door
giving access to
aviary

perches suspended
across flight

flight 1

bins
for
storage
and
waste

service
corridor

nesting area with
box, perches, food
and water

access hole for birds between house
and flight may be closed from outside
using rope and pulley

flight 2

windows

supplied
with heat
and light

lights
on
dimmers

flight 3

brick or wood
with solid roof

clear or semi-opaque roof
(usually plastic)

mesh roof over
flight area

A bank of aviaries with an access corridor attached to one side.

Floor

Parrot keepers use many alternatives on the floor of their aviaries. Bare earth or turf will allow natural foraging or digging activity for species such as Galah (roseate) cockatoos, Grass parakeets or Slender-billed conures *(Enicognathus leptorhynchus)* However, intestinal parasites will be acquired in this way, as well as some infectious diseases. Birds kept in this manner should receive regular prophylactic worming treatments three to four times a year. Earth floors will also allow vermin such as rats to dig their way into the flight and kill its occupants, unless the foundations are dug out and wire mesh is buried under the replaced soil.

Roseate cockatoo, or Galah (Eolophus roseicapillus), *a species that naturally spends a lot of time foraging for food on the ground. This makes it vulnerable to roundworm infestation, as it will ingest the eggs of these parasites from the soil.*

Slender-billed conure (Enicognathus leptorhynchus) *showing the long slender upper beak used for digging for plant roots and bulbs, or winkling out seeds from cones. (Photo: Tony Pittman)*

A well-constructed garden aviary for parakeets. There is an access corridor along the back, sharing the roof with the covered section of the flights that contain the feed bowls and nest boxes. The outer sections of the flights have open roofs, allowing the birds to sit in the rain. The aviary is well constructed and maintained, sited on paving slabs for ease of cleaning and to reduce the possibility of rats and mice gaining access. The area is attractively planted so that it becomes a part of the garden.

Paving slabs or concrete will prevent animals burrowing in, and also make cleaning out easier – the surface may simply be swept over and hosed down. The material should be laid in a slight slope to allow drainage of excess water. Shingle is an excellent alternative: laid over a weed-suppressing membrane, it may be raked over and hosed down, making cleaning quick and easy. Some people use chipped bark: this has the same easy maintenance as shingle, but is a notorious medium for harbouring potentially pathogenic fungal spores, especially when wet. Neither of these materials will prevent rats getting in, unless wire mesh is laid underneath the substrate.

Alternatives are suspended flights. These have the advantage that waste food and droppings will pass through on to the ground underneath, where the birds cannot reach it, making hygiene and disease control very easy. Their disadvantages are difficulty of access to retrieve a bird if required; or the replacement of perches, especially if the flights are large. A 'trapdoor' of mesh in the floor of the flight will enable one to stand head and shoulders into the flight, but the size and layout should make it possible to reach all corners of the flight with a net. Otherwise the bird will be un-catchable.

Suspended flights raised above the ground on brick or wooden supports. These have the advantage that droppings and waste food will drop through to the ground or floor below, reducing the risk of infection to the birds and making cleaning easier. Their disadvantage is that access to the flights is difficult, for example to catch a bird or change perches. The larger the flight, the more difficulty there will be.

Swinging perches suspended on ropes or chains, rope toys, or branches of (non-toxic) trees will give your parrots hours of fun, exercise and stimulation.

Eucalyptus branches, twigs and leaves are particular favourites with parrots. They will enjoy stripping the leaves and the bark.

Perches

The flight should be equipped with perches, placed so as to allow the birds to fly the length of the flight without hindrance, but providing landing places to reach food, water, and the entrance to the 'inner sanctum'. Perches may be fixed rigidly to the wire mesh or the aviary framework, or they may be suspended on chains or ropes from the roof – in fact rope suspended as a loop makes a perfectly adequate perch. Such mobile perches give the active birds more stimulation and exercise, and more closely mimic the living tree branches that parrots would use in the wild. Suitable woods and other materials are discussed in more detail below, but fresh-cut branches of trees such as willow or eucalyptus will give your birds hours of amusement and stimulation.

Plants

Planting of the aviary is contentious. Most parrots will rapidly destroy anything that is growing within the flight; however some planting will not only improve the aesthetic appearance of the flight but will also give the birds physical stimulation. Rapidly growing and regenerating trees or shrubs like willow *(Salix* spp.*)*, elder, mallow or buddleia may survive the onslaught; or the shrubs may be planted outside the wire so that the birds can eat only the branches that grow through, yet are not able to destroy the whole plant. Rapidly growing non-toxic climbing plants such as *Polygonum* species may be used in the same way – rooted outside the aviary but growing over and through it, providing shade, camouflage, and fun for the birds.

Another choice is to plant tubs or pots, and move these in rotation in and out of the flights, giving them time to recover and regenerate on the outside. Old branches or tree trunks, barrels or boxes will also keep your birds amused for hours.

Communal Flight

If space and money allow, and you keep several birds, it is a good idea to have a large communal flight. This will allow the birds to exercise and flock together, encouraging natural parrot behaviour. Young birds that you may have bred, or just recently acquired, can grow together and learn parrot social skills. Older birds that you may wish to breed from may choose their own mates from the group. You can then separate them off into breeding aviaries, knowing that they are far more likely to be a compatible pair than a cock and hen that are simply thrown together. Once again, it is all about providing as good a lifestyle

A communal flight containing a number of cockatoos that are caged indoors overnight and in bad weather, but allowed into the flight for exercise and fresh air when weather is good. The parrots benefit so much from the facility to exercise and explore a new environment: their plumage, fitness, general health and mental wellbeing all improve, and they become less likely to show 'bad' behaviour indoors.

as possible for your birds. You are responsible for their welfare, and they are totally dependent upon you.

Food and Water

Food and water bowls should be accessible, easy cleaned and replaced, and mounted in a sheltered area that the birds can reach easily but vermin cannot – either in the shed section or under the roofed part of the flight. The different types of bowl and fixings available are covered in more detail below.

Nest Boxes

Nest boxes will be required if your parrots are to breed, but this subject will be covered in more detail in Chapter 7.

Maintenance

Daily tasks should include an inspection of the birds (see the story about Jack on page 78). Food and water need to be replaced daily – even more often in hot weather – with bowls washed and disinfected. The aviary should be checked for signs of damage by its occupants, vermin, or the weather.

Weekly tasks will involve cleaning and replacement or repair of perches; checking for signs of vermin; and raking over or hosing down the floor of the aviary.

Annual attention may mean the replacement or repair of nest boxes; treating woodwork with bird-safe preservative; replacing worn locks, hinges, or window fasteners; pruning any overgrown plants that the birds may have left; renewing shingle or bark on the floor; and checking the integrity of roofing materials.

KEEPING INDOOR BIRDS

Most keepers of pet parrots house their cherished companions with them indoors. This allows contact with the bird for the greater part of the parrot's and the owner's lifestyle. There is an obvious advantage to the close proximity and relationship with the pet parrot, who can become a much-loved

Yellow-backed chattering lory (Lorius garrulus) *enjoying being part of indoor family life.*

family member. The bird and its interesting behaviour can be enjoyed and observed at close quarters. The risk of theft is much reduced. However, as with the aviary bird situation, there are also disadvantages to this way of life.

Reducing Length of Day

There is often an artificial extension of the bird's day. Most parrots come from tropical or subtropical latitudes, and as such are accustomed to an approximately twelve-hour cycle of night and day, as experienced on the equator. In a busy household, with family members rising early for school or work, but not retiring to bed until eleven or twelve at night, the bird is exposed year-round to an unnaturally long day. This will stress the bird, and could result in problems such as feather-plucking or irritability.

This problem may be compensated for in part by 'quiet periods' during the day, when all humans are out of the house. In fact, this will approximate the natural diurnal pattern of the wild parrot, which is active and feeding at dawn and dusk, but quiet and resting during the heat of the day.

The bird's cage may also be covered in the evening to allow it to sleep before its owners do, although if left in the same room, most birds will not fully relax. It is therefore worth considering putting the bird in a night cage in a quiet room. However, it must be said that most working owners will want to spend these few hours in the evening having contact with their parrot.

Moist Atmosphere

Houses have a warm, dry atmosphere. Most parrots come from areas of high natural rainfall, and an arid atmosphere is damaging to a bird's plumage.

It is therefore important not to site the parrot's cage too close to a radiator or other heat source; to use a humidifier in the room; and to spray or bathe the bird regularly. Most clients are scared to spray their birds in the winter 'in case they catch cold'. This will not happen! Birds do not 'catch cold'. It is true that they are susceptible to respiratory problems, associated with dietary deficiencies,

environmental irritants, and infectious diseases, but they will not get these by getting wet!

A human home is warm, especially in the winter, and birds should be routinely sprayed with plain warm water three to four times a week to keep the plumage in good condition. In the summer months, this frequency may be increased to daily, or even several times a day, while the parrots will undoubtedly benefit from having some time in a cage outdoors or in an outside flight.

So many of the feather problems we see in parrots are the result of prolonged dry-heat damage and insufficient moisture on their plumage. Parrots will attempt to bathe in their water bowls – this is telling you that the bird is desperate for a bath. They particularly will indulge in this behaviour when there are loud noises around – the vacuum cleaner perhaps, or raucous music. This is because in nature parrots are accustomed to tropical rainstorms and the associated noises of thunder, plus rain drumming on foliage. At these times, parrots will expect to get wet, and will enjoy spreading their wings and hanging upside down in the rain. Amazons especially will behave in this way when sprayed.

Take your pet in the shower with you: perches are available for this very purpose that will attach to tiled walls with rubber suckers. Sit him in the sink with the tap on, or use a fine mist from the

Shower perch for a parrot, mounted to the wall of the cubicle with suckers. The perch section will swivel through 180°.

Hen Eclectus parrot enjoying a shower in the open air, but still secure in her cage.

garden hose while out in the garden – anything to supply a regular soaking bath! Commercial additives are available as 'plumage conditioners', and these may be used periodically, but the routine spray need be just plain warm water. After all, that is what these parrots would be receiving in nature, from the rain clouds above!

Skippy, a Roseate cockatoo, enjoying a shower.

Umbrella cockatoo Indie (Cacatua alba) enjoying a bath in the kitchen sink.

Rock pebbler (Polytelus anthopeplus) Susie Q helping with the washing up!

Jez and Merlin, black-headed caiques (Pionites melanocephala) on a play-stand hanging in the kitchen. Whilst this may allow the birds to be in the centre of human activity, the kitchen is not the safest place for parrots, apart from bath-time. Boiling water, electrical appliances, and cooking fumes are all potential hazards to pet birds.

Household Hazards

There are many potential dangers to a parrot in the average household. These are inquisitive birds, and notorious chewers, and will investigate telephone

Skippy again, exploring the microwave oven. Not the best place for a bird to be; the toaster is also nearby.

cables and power leads. Building plaster, paintwork and metal objects are all possible sources of danger. Quality curtains may have lead sewn in their lower hems to weigh them down, and curious birds may pick out this metal and swallow it. They will eat the leaves of houseplants, so ensure you do not keep any poisonous varieties anywhere near your birds!

The long-suffering Brodie (Jack Russell terrier) sacrificing his place on the sofa to budgerigar Ollie.

Peach-fronted conure (Aratinga aurea) Peachie attempting to share a glass of wine – another potential hazard of keeping pet birds in the home!

A stand-off between Umbrella cockatoo Dougal and tabby kitten George. The distance between them is as close as they would approach comfortably – any closer and fur and feathers would fly! Under close supervision, these two will test the other's reactions and will develop respect for each other.

Other pets in the household may at best be a nuisance to the parrot, and at worst could seriously damage or kill it. Having said that, the majority of dogs and cats will learn a healthy respect for a parrot once they have experienced the power of that beak!

Toxic Fumes

Perhaps the most serious of the household hazards relates to toxic fumes. As explained in Chapter 1, birds have a highly efficient respiratory system in order to absorb the extra oxygen needed to power flight muscles, but any gas will be rapidly absorbed – not just oxygen. That is why canaries were used in coal mines as detectors of methane and carbon monoxide. They would fall off their perches long before these gases built up sufficiently to harm humans.

Therefore any noxious material in the atmosphere of the home will affect your birds. Cigarette smoke, scented candles, incense burners, open fires, aerosol sprays – all will cause irritation to your birds' lungs and air-sacs, and chronic exposure can result in permanent damage. This problem is no better illustrated than by a post-mortem examination I carried out some years ago on a much-loved Amazon parrot.

The mostly deadly of toxic fumes are associated with cooking. Over-heated cooking oil will release a blue smoke that will soon cause a parrot to gasp and choke, so be careful of those deep fat fryers and heating the wok for the stir-fry. Self-cleaning ovens

that work at high temperatures, new grill pans, or Teflon®-coated saucepans will all – if over-heated or allowed to burn dry – release toxic fumes that will make us cough and our eyes run, but will kill a parrot in minutes.

Many times over the years I have seen this happen: parrots perfectly healthy and happy one minute will suddenly start to gasp and cough, then collapse on the floor with wings spread, and die moments later. Post-mortem examination reveals a distinctive bright cherry-red colour to the lungs, as the lung tissue is invaded with red blood cells. One particular case involved several birds in a household that lived in different rooms. Those nearest the kitchen when a saucepan boiled dry died within five minutes; those in the next room took ten minutes before they succumbed. Of three birds kept upstairs, one died thirty minutes later; and the other two survived, but had serious breathing problems for several days afterwards.

The home can be a dangerous place for birds!

Type of Cage

If your parrot is going to spend most of its life in a cage, then this home should be as large as you can afford and accommodate in your house. It is a legal requirement that the bird should at least be able to fully spread its wings in all directions.

African grey parrot in a cage suitable only for a budgerigar. As a legal minimum the bird should at least be able to extend its wings fully in all three dimensions. The more time the bird spends in its cage, the larger it should be.

SHADY PAST

Yellow-headed Amazon (Amazona ochrocephala oratrix). *(Photo: Jan Hooimeijer DVM)*

Popeye was a mature Yellow-headed Amazon *(Amazona ochrocephala oratrix)* of some thirty-five years, and a wonderful character. He had an extensive vocabulary of words, but also sounds such as telephone and doorbells, laughing and crying, coughing and sneezing. Unlike many talking birds, he loved an audience, and would go through his repertoire to order. His owner for the last five years of his life was a lovely lady who used Popeye as entertainment at children's parties, where he was always a great hit because of his mimicry and guaranteed performance.

Mrs Hooper was understandably devastated when one day Popeye suddenly fell off his perch and died, with no previous signs of illness. Because of the unexpectedness of this event, and because she had other birds in the house, Mrs Hooper rightly decided to have me carry out a post-mortem examination on her bird.

All his air-sac membranes (which should be thin and transparent) were thickened and cloudy, and dotted with black spots of soot. The lungs were congested, and also filled with black spots. This is known as anthracosis, and is the result of accumulation of hydrocarbon particles from cigarette smoke in the respiratory system. In addition, the major vessels leading from the heart were yellow and thickened with fatty deposits, known as atherosclerosis. This obviously has the effect of reducing the diameter and elasticity of these arteries, thus increasing the load on the heart.

This pathology is the direct result of the inhalation of tobacco smoke, and Popeye ultimately died of heart failure because of the long-term damage sustained in this way. Mrs Hooper was devastated. She and her family were confirmed non-smokers. How could this have happened?

As I have said, Popeye was owned by this family for just the last five years. Questioning revealed that his previous owner had owned a pub, and for the first thirty years of his life, Popeye had lived in the public bar! He was thus subject to passive smoking on a grand scale, with the unfortunate result described. Although he had lived latterly in a clean environment, the damage to his system was already done, with irreversible and fatal consequences.

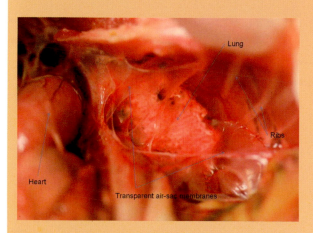

Post-mortem dissection of a parrot showing the left thoracic air sac. The normal membranes are thin and transparent, whereas those found in Popeye were thickened, cloudy, and dotted with black spots of soot.

Blue and yellow macaw displaying its impressive wingspan and bright colours. Parrots need to stretch their limbs and flap their wings so need sufficient space.

A large parrot cage on display in a pet store. Note the opening top with a perch for the bird to sit out on, the inverted 'skirt' of metal to catch dropped food items, the legs on castors to make the cage more manoeuvrable, and an additional drawer for storage under the cage-bottom tray.

The selection of cage type follows many of the criteria involved with building aviaries. It should be appropriate in size, strength and wire gauge for the species of bird and the number of occupants. It should be manoeuvrable and easily dismantled for cleaning and maintenance. Cages on wheels or castors are therefore easier to manage than those with plain legs. The bird can then be moved from room to room with its owners, or out in to the garden or conservatory for a change of scenery.

Ornate and fancy curlicues such as those favoured by our Victorian ancestors may look attractive, but make danger points where birds may get their toes or other extremities trapped. Simple but strong construction, with ease of access to the bird, perches, and bowls are paramount. There is a plethora of styles and shapes on the market, some of which are illustrated here. Having selected a type appropriate to your bird, the final choice will depend on how it will fit in your home and your personal preference of colour and material.

A variety of cages in various styles and finishes. Most are of reasonable size, and on castors to make movement easier. The final picture is a smaller cage with a plastic tray and carrying handle, and should not be used for anything other than temporary housing, transport, or as a night cage.

Cockatoo, in a wire basket pet carrier, useful for transport such as going to the vet's clinic.

The bird's home cage is its primary dwelling where it may be left safe and secure while the owners are out, but a second, smaller cage may be used as a spare while you clean your pet's regular home, or it could be used for him to sleep in at night or to take out into the garden. Finally, you may also consider a travel carrier, to make transporting the parrot to the vet's clinic or holiday boarding easier.

Cleaning and Disinfection

'Birds in the wild don't have their branches scrubbed with disinfectant' is an often-quoted comment by bird-owners wishing to do less work. Of course they don't, but they also do not sit on the same piece of branch day after day, week after week, with waste food and droppings accumulating all around them! Native leaves and branches are washed regularly by heavy rainfall, and many microbes are killed by the ultraviolet rays in sunlight. Pet indoor birds on the other hand are restricted to a comparatively small area, and we have a duty of care to our birds to prevent the build-up of dirt and potential infection.

Some cages have a grid floor above the base tray, which allows waste food and bird droppings to pass through. The bird cannot then reach discarded food to pick it up and attempt to eat it, thus avoiding the risk of potential contamination. This is good idea in principle, but wasteful of food: most parrots will sort through their food bowls, searching for favourite items and evicting the rest, but will go down to the discarded items later in the day. There is also a potential danger in getting feet or wings caught in the grid, especially if the bird panics for some reason.

There are many possible materials to cover a solid cage or play-stand base. People use cat litter, dried corn waste, compressed paper granules, wood or bark chippings or sawdust, plastic floor

Cage base showing a removable tray lined with newspaper mounted below a wire grid. This allows waste food and droppings to fall through onto the paper, out of the parrot's reach, thereby reducing the risk of ingesting contaminated material. The owner can clear away the waste easily by withdrawing the tray and replacing the newspaper.

coverings, or sheets of paper. But be advised: free access to a cage floor or play-stand tray covered with cat litter, woodchip, or sawdust is an open invitation for the parrot to scatter these materials around your room! Chipped bark is also a common source of disease-causing fungal spores, especially when damp, so is best avoided.

By far the simplest technique is to cover the floor with several layers of old newspapers. The top page may be removed each day, taking with it the discarded debris and droppings, and leaving the next clean sheet. Once a week, the whole cage, tray and perches should be dismantled, washed, disinfected with an avian-safe product, rinsed, dried, and replaced. Plastic, wood, or metal toys should be treated in the same way; rope toys may be washed and dried; while cardboard is simply thrown away.

Food and Water Bowls

Eating and drinking bowls, on the other hand, should be cleaned thoroughly every day. Parrots delight in dunking their food in their drinking water, and carelessly placed perches result in easy contamination of bowls with droppings. Fruits and vegetables will deteriorate rapidly in warm weather, and accumulated waste food and droppings will rapidly form a rich culture medium for pathogenic bacteria and fungi.

Whatever type of dish is used, this need for daily cleaning and replenishing has led to some ingenious designs to make access easy. The simple plastic D-cup hooks over horizontal bars or wires, for example: their removal necessitates opening the cage or aviary, and they are also removed easily by playful parrots, who will delight in emptying their contents on the floor! The plastic may split, crack, or become scratched. The scratched surface will be difficult to properly sterilize and will harbour germs.

Water bowl contaminated with droppings, as it had been placed directly underneath the bird's perch.

D-cup on the door of a parrot's cage showing a 'bacterial soup' of dirty water, with droppings and seed debris. In warm weather this will rapidly become a dangerous source of infection to your bird. (Photo: Jan Hooimeijer DVM)

Plastic D-cup hooked over the bars of a cage. This is perhaps the simplest variety of food and water bowl, cheap and easy to remove and replace – but therefore also easy for the parrot to unhook and empty all over the floor!

Stainless steel coop cups are more substantial, longer lasting, and much easier to clean and disinfect thoroughly. They also hook over cage bars – and therefore may be dislodged by a mischievous bird, unless the holder is held in place with wire or a spring clip.

Stainless steel coop cups are similarly suspended, but are more robust and generally easier to keep clean. The holding brackets may be wired to the cage to make them more difficult for the parrot to remove. Other cages have an opening in their construction that will receive a hard plastic cup that is then secured in place using a clip on the outside of the cage.

The final choice, especially useful in larger cages or aviaries, is a rotating mechanism whereby access to the bowls is achieved by rotating the holder from outside the cage. Bowls may be removed, cleaned, replenished and replaced, and are usually locked in position by various means, before rotating the holding mechanism back inside the cage.

A rotating metal mechanism built into the cage mesh, which may be turned round to release the food bowls from outside the cage or aviary. The rotating panel may be locked in place from outside, and there is usually a lip or flange on the inside to prevent parrots lifting the bowls out of their holding rings.

Plastic D-cups that fit a specific opening in the cage, and are held in place with a wire clip. Artful parrots may still be able to undo these clips and push out the dishes, so the clips have been secured here with spring clips. This system has the advantage that the dishes may be removed and replaced from outside the cage, unlike D-cups or coop cups which require the cage door to be opened.

CHAPTER 5

Enriching the Environment

As stated in the previous chapter, the parrot's home cage should be as large as you can accommodate and afford, and it will provide a safe and secure environment while owners are out.

PERCHES

However, some freedom from this cage is desirable when owners are at home, to give the bird physical exercise and mental stimulation. This may be achieved by something as simple as an opening top to the cage, across which may be suspended a perch with attached toys or bowls.

A simple T-perch on a stand allows the bird some freedom and socialization, and the owner can move the stand around the house or out into

the garden. Larger wooden or metal stands may be purpose-made or purchased, or swings and ropes may be suspended in a corner of the room. Java wood is an excellent choice for the perch, being extremely hard and virtually indestructible to a parrot's beak, while existing in tortuous shapes to provide good climbing and gripping exercise.

That is not to say that parrots should not be given soft wood to destroy. It is a natural part of their behaviour; it keeps them physically and mentally stimulated, and is of benefit in keeping the beak in trim. I have discussed the use of natural wood perches with my clients on many occasions, only to be told 'Oh I have tried that, but he chews

This cage has a triangular metal framework incorporated into its top, and mounted over a metal tray. The frame supports a perch with ladder and food bowls, so that the parrot may be placed outside of its cage onto the perch. There is a detachable perch made of 'java' wood in the foreground.

Hinged wire panels at the top of this cage may be opened and a perch fixed across the opening, allowing the parrot to climb out and sit on top.

These cages in the bird-room of a pet store are equipped with 'play-stands', mounted with a variety of toys, to allow their inmates some freedom and play time while waiting for a suitable purchaser.

through it and destroys it inside a week'. So what? At least he is not chewing his own feathers or skin, or systematically destroying your home!

It is easy enough to replace perches on a regular basis with parrot-safe wood. Hazel (*Corylus*), birch (*Betula*), chestnut (*Castanea*), sycamore and

Galah Skippy showing off on a wooden perch supported on an enamelled metal stand.

Green-winged macaw (Ara chloroptera) *above, and Scarlet macaw* (Ara macao) *below, in a corner of their bird-room, with swings of rope, plastic and chain suspended from the ceiling.*

maple (*Acer*), eucalyptus, and any untreated fruit tree branches are all fine. So are willow (*Salix*), mallow (*Lavatera*), elder (*Sambucus*) and buddleia, and these rapidly growing species will regenerate swiftly after cutting, so you are not doing serious damage to the environment. Branches may be scrubbed free of bird-droppings, lichen, or moss, and cut to size to fit the cage.

Actively toxic plants such as Yew (*Taxus baccata*), Laburnum (*Laburnum*) or Lilac (*Syringa*) should obviously not be used. I usually avoid oak (*Quercus robur*) and beech (*Fagus sylvatica*) because of

Jez and Merlin on a chromium-plated perch in their garden. Note again the zygodactyl toes of parrots (two forward and two back), and the colourful plumage and mischievous attitude of these characterful birds (Black-headed caiques – Pionites melanocephala).

A trio of macaws of different sizes on a plastic and wood play perch. From left to right – Military macaw (Ara militaris), Chestnut-fronted or Severe macaw (Ara severa), and a Scarlet macaw (Ara macao). Note again the zygodactyl toes, large hooked bills, round fleshy tongues and colourful plumage typical of the parrot family.

tannins in their bark, and pine trees because of the high resin content. Sawn pine off-cuts (where the bark has been removed) from a timber merchant are fine as long as they have not been treated with a chemical preservative.

The perches supplied with most cages, of the smooth wooden dowel or broom-handle variety, or of plastic tubing, may be easy to keep clean but they are not good for birds' feet for lifelong perching.

Young Blue Fronted Amazon and African Grey parrots on play stands.

Two play stands of different sizes, made of java wood and mounted on a wooden tray to catch droppings and scattered food.

Close-up of a java wood stand, showing attachment of toys
and bowls via screw-eyes and chains.

Saxo, Sulphur-crested cockatoo (Cacatua sulphurea): 'Do
you really expect me to sit up here and not chew?' These
birds are naturally inquisitive and their beaks are made to
re-model wood, so do not be surprised if they do exactly that
to woodwork in your home, if allowed the freedom.

It is far better to provide your parrot with natural, safe wood
like this branch of eucalyptus from which this Long-billed
corella (Cacatua tenuirostris) here is having a great time
stripping the twigs, leaves, and bark.

Birds require a variety in diameter, texture, and
hardness: their toes, feet and joints will be much
better for it, while the ability to chew a natural
wood perch will satisfy their natural instincts and
provide excellent environmental enrichment.

So-called 'pedicure' perches, made of a con-
crete-like compound with a rough sandy texture
intended to 'file down' the tips of the bird's claws
as it perches are useful for that purpose, but it
is wrong to make all the parrot's perches of this
material. This would lead to sores on the sole
of the foot. Most available perches should be of
wood, with just one – perhaps sited near a food
or water bowl – of the pedicure type. But why do
manufacturers make them in such bright colours?
I have seen many an African grey parrot terrified
when expected to sit on a new pedicure perch in
bright pink or blue!

The sandpaper sheaths supplied to slip over the
doweling perches of budgerigar cages, for the same
principle of nail care, are fine for these small birds,

Smooth dowelling or 'broom-handle' type of perch supplied with most commercial parrot cages. This type of perch is not good for the bird's feet in the long-term – they need more variety of diameter and texture. Note the blue aluminium leg ring for identification on this African grey parrot, and the grey iris of the eye, denoting a very young bird.

'Pedicure perch' manufactured from a coloured cement-like mix, with a sandy texture. The surface is intended to provide grip, as well as keeping the nail tips from becoming too sharp. In the cage are two Peach-faced lovebirds (Agapornis roseicollis).

but are a complete waste of time for larger parrots. They will be ripped to shreds in seconds.

TOYS

An essential part of parrot welfare is to provide these intelligent birds with something to keep them physically and mentally occupied. It is often repeated that these birds have the level of understanding of a four to five-year-old child. Their attention span is of a similar level, but they will learn quickly, and will get bored if not given something to do. This boredom will result in behavioural problems such as feather-plucking or self-mutilation, screaming, or damage to the owner's home and furnishings.

Increasing awareness of this need for environmental enrichment for pet parrots has led to an explosion in the market of parrot toys. These toys may be made from wood, metal, plastic, leather or rope. The wood is often brightly coloured, but make sure the dyes used are simple vegetable-based colourings, and non-toxic. Plastics should

Length of chain from a parrot toy. The separate link had become embedded in a macaw's beak, and had to be removed under anaesthetic. Ensure that such chains are strong enough not to be dismantled by your parrot, and that the links and clasps are made of stainless steel rather than galvanized metal, which is a potential source of zinc poisoning.

be hard and virtually indestructible: any that are child-safe will be fine for your bird. Metal chains, links, or bells should be stainless steel, in preference to cheaper galvanized materials which would bring the risk of zinc poisoning, but be aware of the possibility of beaks and toes getting caught in the links or cracks.

Apart from being safe, toys should be cheap and interesting. One can spend a fortune on manufactured toys, which the parrot may either ignore completely, or destroy in a few minutes! Cheaper versions (provided they are safe) can be readily replaced, thus maintaining your bird's interest. However, many parrots (especially African greys) can be wary of new items, so you may have to introduce the toy (or new perch, food bowl, or food item...) slowly before he will accept it. Place the new item near the cage, where the bird can see it, but not too close to be intimidating. Move it progressively closer until it is hanging on the outside of the cage, and then eventually try placing it inside.

Saxo again, not doing as much damage to the chair as she has to the door in the picture on page 99, but playing with a nearly empty juice carton. She has learned to tilt the container to allow any remain juice to run down into her mouth. Such simple, cheap and replaceable toys will keep parrots amused, and will distract them from damaging the home or their feathers.

Similarly with cardboard rolls from kitchen paper towel or toilet tissue. Eric would enjoy tearing such items to shreds. Several such rolls could be threaded onto a length of rope or chain and suspended in the cage to make a cheap plaything.

to 'fit in' to a degree with the human owner's lifestyle. But these birds are not like domesticated cats and dogs, that have lived with human beings for many, many generations, and have become genetically modified and 'domesticated' in the process, so that they are now largely dependent upon human beings for their wellbeing. Captive parrots (apart from budgerigars, grass parakeets and cockatiels) are just a few generations away from being wild birds, and as such we should as far as possible try to mimic and provide for their natural lifestyle, rather than imposing too much of our own on them, nor expecting too much of them.

This is not to say that parrots will not learn basic guidelines such as mealtimes, bedtime, playtime or areas that are out of bounds and behaviour that is unacceptable. It is good for children and sentient animals to have 'house rules'. But this should not be taken to extremes. In the wild, parrots will awake with the dawn, communicate loudly with their family and flock, and then fly off to forage for

Apart from the pleasure and occupation parrots will get from hanging and swinging on the toys, and trying to dismantle them, the toys may be used to encourage the bird's problem-solving abilities. Favourite food items may be partially concealed within the toy, so the parrot is encouraged to work out how to remove them. Simple, replaceable, items of this type may be made at home – such things as cardboard roll cores from kitchen towels or toilet paper, breakfast cereal or tissue boxes, or papier-mâché egg boxes are all suitable for this purpose.

ROUTINE – IS IT NECESSARY?

Just like young children, puppies or kittens, parrots need to be aware of ground-rules and limitations in the household. All these animals will quickly learn the meaning of words like 'no', 'not', 'good bird', 'stop', 'bad', 'well done' and the like, when used appropriately and in context.

Pet parrots are inherently wild animals maintained in an alien environment, and as such need

STICKING TO THE ROUTINE!

At my clinic we have in the past done parrot-boarding for clients, and many a cherished pet has come in with pages of instructions such as:

He has a couple of spoonfuls of breakfast cereal with milk at 8:00 in the morning, then he has to have his digestive biscuit dunked in tea at 10:30. He always has a square of toast with low-fat spread at 12:15, and then he joins me for a cream cracker and cheese at 3:20. At ten to six we give him a one-inch square of coconut, and then just before we put him to bed at 9:30 he has two peanuts in shell.

A degree of timetable is useful to the parrot, but not at this level of accuracy! It is not necessary to follow it to the letter every day. Often routine has been made by the owner to suit their own personalities rather than having any major advantage to the bird.

food. The middle hours of the day (generally the hottest time) are spent quietly resting, preening, bathing, or playing. Foraging and feeding again take place in the late afternoon, before the birds return to their roosting area, chatter again, and settle down to sleep for the night.

It is therefore normal for pet parrots to be noisy and active, and to want to eat, at the beginning and end of the day, while they will rest or perhaps play in the middle, and want to settle to sleep at dusk. This degree of 'routine' is fine, but it is not necessary to take such routine to extremes.

ULTRAVIOLET LIGHT

It is generally true that outdoor birds have much better quality plumage than their indoor cousins. There is more sheen to the feathers; with brighter, more vivid colours. This is a reflection of the general health benefits of more exercise, fresh air, soaking with rainwater, and exposure to sunlight. The ultraviolet (UV) wavelengths in sunlight are essential for the synthesis of vitamin D in the skin and the preen gland (where present). Parrots kept indoors have the same requirement, and if kept permanently inside will eventually suffer 'sunlight deficiency'. As described earlier, the dry, warm indoor atmosphere and a lack of opportunity for bathing will result in dull dusty plumage.

There is absolutely no doubt that indoor pet birds will benefit from exposure to fresh air and sunshine, weather permitting. It is therefore well worth taking your pets outside on a sunny day where possible. Their plumage will take on a healthy sheen with enhanced colouring. Such exposure may also be achieved by taking the bird out attached to its owner by means of a safe bird harness, or leash attached to a leg ring. Such items should only ever be used for short periods, and only when the owner is present to supervise. The bird should never be left on its own, tethered to a tree or fence. I have seen many accidents result from such treatment, where a bird has been startled or tried to fly away, or has simply been playing while harnessed. The result of such an accident may be broken legs or wings, or even strangulation and death.

Blue and yellow macaw (Ara ararauna) *enjoying the great outdoors. Note the sheen on the plumage – always much better on birds that live outside rather than in a warm, dry, indoor atmosphere. This bird has a stainless steel identity ring on its leg.*

A Dutch veterinary colleague of mine encourages his clients to take their birds out together on 'parrot picnics', where not only do they all benefit from the open air and sunshine, but they have the opportunity to socialize with other birds and people.

A safer alternative is to take the bird out in a small carry cage, such as is used for its sleep at night, or general transport. Even then, the cage

A 'parrot picnic' in The Netherlands, where families and their pet parrots can have a fun day out in the open air, and birds are allowed to socialize. (Photo: Jan Hooimeijer DVM)

should not be left unattended in the garden, as marauding cats, dogs, children or birds of prey may startle the bird, tip over its cage, or even cause the cage to open so that the bird escapes. A bird needs only twenty minutes of exposure to UV light in order to manufacture its daily requirement of vitamin D_3. (Some is also supplied directly in the diet.) Thus a short period outdoors is all that is necessary.

If there really is no opportunity to get the bird out of the home (apartments with no gardens, birds that get too scared by being outside, or during the winter months and prolonged inclement weather), then UVB radiation may be given by using avian-specific ultraviolet light sources. To be effective, these need to be mounted quite close to the parrot: they will do nothing if mounted on the ceiling or across the other side of the room.

However, once again twenty minutes exposure in a day is ample to supply the bird's needs. Leaving such lights switched on in such close proximity for prolonged periods (twelve hours a day, every day) can cause damage to their eyes – I have seen a number of birds develop cataracts in such conditions.

Magpie (Pica pica) *anaesthetized and intubated in preparation for removing the cataract (opaque lens) from the eye.*

TO COVER THE CAGE OR NOT?

I have mentioned earlier that parrots need a good twelve hours sleep in every twenty-four, and covering the cage at night may assist that when owners are up and active. A better option is to place the bird in a small night cage in a quiet room to get its rest. Many owners of indoor parrots will cover their pets' cages at night time; many do not. Either way the birds seem content. It is natural for a parrot to seek a sheltered place (usually in foliage) to roost and sleep at night, and obviously once the sun goes down, they will be in darkness. As mentioned previously, artificially prolonged daylight hours in the human household are not good for the bird; therefore covering the cage to allow him to sleep is a good idea.

On the other hand, if you cover your bird simply to 'keep him warm and out of a draught', then there really is no need! He was perfectly warm and comfortable during the day, so why should he be any different at night? In nature, birds will roost overnight in temperatures well below those they experience during daylight hours. Feathers are excellent insulators – your own feather-filled duvet or eiderdown keeps you snug in bed, and it will do the same for your pet. As I have said before, birds will not 'catch cold' by being in a draught. They will be uncomfortable and miserable if wet and cold, therefore they should not be bathed or sprayed before retiring, but they can put up with the odd draught!

If you do cover your bird's cage, then ensure the fabric used is non-toxic. Most parrots will work at the material with their beaks and toes, pulling it through the bars to shred it and chew it.

Covering a screeching parrot simply to give the owner some peace may temporarily quieten it down, but this 'punishment' should not be used repeatedly to control this common and difficult problem. Better management methods will be discussed in Chapter 10.

CHAPTER 6

Providing a Balanced Diet

For many years captive parrots were fed a mixture of dried seeds – 'parrot mix' for the larger species, and 'parakeet mix' for the smaller ones. These mixtures included small grass seeds, millets, oats, wheat, dried corn, safflower, sunflower, and usually pine nuts and peanuts (groundnuts). These seed mixes are still actively promoted by the pet trade as being 'a balanced diet' for parrots, and traditional bird-keepers are reluctant to consider any alternatives.

As we found in Chapters 1 and 2 however, there are thousands of parrot species in a wide variety of shapes and sizes and indigenous to many different environments. It is therefore unreasonable to suppose that this 'one size fits all' philosophy could possibly work. Broadly speaking, parrots may be divided into grain eaters, including seeds, nuts and beans (like budgerigars and parakeets); fruit eaters (like most Amazon parrots and Eclectus); and specialist nectar eaters (lories and lorikeets).

Other domesticated species have had their dietary requirements extensively researched for many decades, and we are well-used to feeding proprietary formulated diets to puppies, kittens, geriatric dogs and cats, kidney patients, horses, cattle, even koi carp. All have their own specially-prepared diets containing their required nutrients in exact percentages.

The standard 'parrot mix' – a mixture of dried seeds, grains and nuts. Seen here are black-and-white striped sunflower seeds, white safflower, small brown pine nuts, dried maize (sweetcorn), cereal grains and dried legumes, peanuts, dried chilli, possibly currants, and a lot of dusty debris. Such a mix may be of variable quality, and it is high in carbohydrate and fat content but very low in essential vitamins and minerals.

The standard 'parakeet' mix, sold for smaller parrots including cockatiels. This mix also contains sunflower and safflower, with cereal grains, round brown seeds of hemp, and smaller millet and other seeds.

A pair of Lories in a bird park, taking nectar mix from a visitor. These birds feed on pollens and nectars from flowers, and have a specially adapted brush-tipped tongue to aid the collection of this food. (See also page 123.)

Dietary research on avian species, on the other hand, until recently has fallen far behind. The nutritional requirements for domesticated poultry have been well-documented because of their

The popular cockatiel (Nymphicus hollandicus). Considerable research has been done on the dietary requirements of this species, but care should be taken in extrapolating the results obtained and applying them to other parrot species.

A seeding grass-head such as many of the small parakeets, including budgerigars, would feed on in their native habitats.

commercial importance in the human food chain. The only other species to have similar research to any extent was the cockatiel *(Nymphicus hollandicus)*. Extrapolating the limited information from chickens and cockatiels to apply to the needs of all other parrot species is obviously fraught with danger and liable to error.

In nature, small parakeets (including budgerigars) from fairly arid areas do in fact feed on seeding grasses, and in times of drought these may approach the dry, mature seeds that we offer in a parakeet mix. However, for much of the year, especially in the breeding season, these birds will take younger, fresher, greener shoots, flowers, and seed heads.

Parrots and parakeets from wetter tropical areas are facultative omnivores – that is, they will feed on pretty much anything and everything that is available and reasonably palatable. They will forage through the rainforest canopy eating buds, shoots, flowers, leaves and fruits as they come into season,

A wild Senegal parrot (Poicephalus senegalus) *feeding on flowers in Africa. Most parrots are opportunist feeders, foraging for whatever fruit, seed, bud, or flower may be in season at the time. (Photo: Nigel Harcourt-Brown MRCVS)*

A group of Green-winged macaws (Ara chloroptera) *and Chestnut-fronted macaws* (Ara severa) *at a clay bank in the Brazilian rainforest. Eating the clay is believed to act as a digestive aid, neutralizing toxins in ingested plant material. (Photo: Steve Brooks)*

as well as the occasional grub or insect. They may gorge themselves on one particular favourite fruit when it is at its peak, but then will move on to another part of their feeding territory and a different plant.

During the course of a year they will take in a wide range of nutrients, generally achieving a natural balance of requirements in that time. There will be lean periods associated with the dry season and plants' growing cycles, alternating with a 'flush' of optimum quality and quantity. This is generally when the birds time their breeding season, so that eggs and the subsequent chicks will receive the best possible sustenance. This is especially obvious in the more temperate arid areas, with marked wet and dry seasons. Poor growing seasons will be reflected in a lack of breeding success. Optimal nutrition is required for growth, breeding, and moulting. Outside of these periods in a bird's life, it is able to survive on 'maintenance rations'.

In captivity, our parrots are dependent upon us to provide them with food of the right quality and quantity at appropriate stages in their lives.

Parrots will select food items according to colour and taste, although they have far fewer taste buds

than do humans. In spite of this, wild parrots do appear to consume plant items that contain mild toxins that are gastro-intestinal irritants. Parrots have been seen gathering in huge numbers at 'clay licks' ingesting clay material from cliff walls. This is believed to provide the birds with a natural 'indigestion agent' to protect their stomach linings from such irritants.

Moluccan cockatoo (Cacatua moluccensis) *eating a grape. This particular bird had lost the tip of his upper beak in the past. It is now healing and growing back, and the bird is still able to perform the delicate task of peeling a soft grape, using its muscular tongue and huge beak.*

Blue and yellow macaw (Ara ararauna) *again holding food (in this case a nut) in its foot, while tongue and beak work on cracking open the shell to reach the kernel.*

There is anatomical and physiological variation in the gastro-intestinal tracts of birds, resulting from their different dietary constituents and digestive processes. Therefore, feeding all parrots the same type of basic mix will obviously create problems.

Parrots are very dextrous with their beaks, muscular tongues, and feet, manipulating and exploring food items, delicately peeling them, or powerfully cracking open thick shells. Lories and lorikeets have a 'brush-tongue' (*see* page 123) with numerous tiny papillae on the tip that increase its surface area, and facilitate the collection of nectar and pollen.

DIETARY REQUIREMENTS

All animals require the following classes of ingredients in their diet to survive, grow, reproduce, and remain healthy.

Fats, Carbohydrates and Proteins

Fats are required as an energy source and for the utilization and storage of fat-soluble vitamins. Recommended levels for parrots are quoted as 2–4 per cent of the total dietary intake, much lower than is needed in productive species like poultry. The level will increase in the laying hen, as egg yolk has a high fat content, providing a valuable energy source to the developing embryo. Large macaws and African grey parrots are known to favour high-fat nuts such as palm nuts. Sunflower seeds, which form a major part of most commercial 'parrot seed mixes', contain 20 per cent fat. These seeds are selectively consumed by parrots (especially African greys) because of their high fat content – just as humans like to eat crisps and chocolate!

Carbohydrates (sugars and starches) provide a rapidly metabolizable energy source, and are the only food constituents utilized by the central nervous system for this purpose. Quantities required vary widely, depending on physical activity,

Palm nuts, oil-rich fruits that are a great favourite with many parrots, especially large macaws and African greys.

Hyacinthine macaws feasting on palm nuts in Brazil. (Photo: Tony Pittman)

environmental temperature, and fat reserves. Free-living parrots in the winter are estimated to require 50 per cent more energy intake than caged indoor birds.

Proteins are the essential 'building blocks' of the body, and are required to form muscle and all other body tissues, including feathers. Again, required levels are lower than those suggested for high-producing species like poultry, but levels of 10–15 per cent of total dietary intake are suggested for maintenance, rising to 20 per cent at times of rapid growth (chicks), egg production, or repair and replacement (recovery from illness or moulting). Seed-based diets are very low in available

protein, and therefore parrots will consume large quantities of seed in an attempt to make up their daily percentage protein requirement, thereby consuming excessive amounts of fats and carbohydrates as well. Nectar feeders gather their protein in the form of flower pollen and some insect matter. When these birds are breeding, they will take animal protein in the form of insects or spiders to provide the higher levels of protein required by their growing chicks. Larger parrots will consume snails, fish, or even carrion for the same reasons.

Proteins are made up of constituent amino acids, which are absorbed after digestion and recombined to form new protein molecules. Some amino acids may be manufactured in the body

The sunflower (Helianthus annuus), *a readily available, prolific producer of the seed forming the bulk of most parrot seed-mixes. It is also oil-rich, and therefore attractive to parrots, but tends to be low in protein, mineral and vitamin content.*

Young Blue and yellow macaw showing a healthy shine to its plumage, with good feather colour, bright eyes and clear nostrils – all signs of general good health and reflecting a nutritionally balanced diet.

from constituent elements (non-essential amino acids), but others *have* to be taken in the diet (essential amino acids). Poor quality or insufficient dietary protein resulting in reduced intake of these essential amino acids will have profound effects on feather quality and colour, chick growth rates, and breeding performance.

Vitamins and Minerals

Vitamins are required for many chemical processes and reactions in the body, and may be divided into fat-soluble (vitamins A, D, E and K), and water-soluble (vitamins B-complex and C). Fat-soluble

The critically endangered Kaka (Nestor meridionalis) from New Zealand, holding a portion of maize (sweetcorn) cob in its foot, while picking off the kernels with its beak and tongue. This bird is one of a captive breeding colony in a protected reserve: note the coloured plastic rings on its leg to make visual identification of individual birds easier; and the aerial visible beside its tail, which is part of a tracking device attached to the tail so that the parrot's movements may be followed.

vitamins are stored in the body, usually in the liver, allowing some latitude in lean times, provided sufficient have been taken in to store. However, this also means there is the potential for over-load if too much is present in the diet – this is encountered commonly with vitamins A and D. Toxic effects – primarily kidney damage – can result from such a situation. Water-soluble vitamins, on the other hand, are excreted from the body without being stored, so any excess in the diet will be expelled. Therefore regular daily intake of these vitamins is required to maintain the bird's needs, and subsequent full health.

Vitamin A will be found in dark green foods (kale, spinach, broccoli, sweet potato, peas and beans), carrot, sweetcorn, peppers, and mango. Vitamin D is manufactured by the bird in its skin and preen gland, in response to ultraviolet radiation (see earlier), but is also present in egg yolk, fish oils and milk. Vitamin E is obtained from spinach, apples and pears, mango, almonds and walnuts, sweet potatoes, sunflower kernels, pine nuts, and wheatgerm. Vitamin K supply comes from green vegetables and eggs, as well as bacteria in the gut. This latter vitamin is especially required by fig parrots *(Opopsitta* and *Psittaculirostris* spp.)*.

Vitamin C is found primarily in apples, oranges, tomatoes, strawberries, kiwi fruit, and rose hips. It is also synthesized by the bird in its liver, so deficiency is rarely a problem. It does, however, enhance the absorption of iron, so too many vitamin C-rich foods may be a problem in birds susceptible to iron-storage disease. Vitamins of the B-group include thiamine (B_1), riboflavin (B_2), niacin, pyridoxine (B_6), biotin, pantothenic acid, folic acid, choline and cyanocobalamin (B_{12}). These are generally obtained from wheatgerm (wholemeal bread), dark greens, eggs, and sunflower.

Minerals are also essential to parrots for several important reasons. Calcium is arguably the most important (or at least the most widely studied), and is present in dark green foods, natural mineral sources such as oyster shell or cuttlefish bone, egg shells, cooked chicken bones, oranges, chick peas, bread or toast, and milk or milk-products such as cheese. It is often reported that parrots should not be given milk as they cannot digest it. This is true

BONES FOR PROTEIN

When I discuss diets for parrots with my clients, and suggest giving cooked chicken bones as a valuable source of calcium and protein, the usual reaction is a grimace and the comment, 'Oh no, that is cannibalistic!' I can understand the reaction – a bird eating a piece of another bird – but strictly speaking, it is not cannibalistic, as this applies only to the same species. Chickens will attack and eat bits of each other, that is true, and very unpleasant. But giving a parrot a cooked chicken leg bone with a little meat on it once in a while does no harm at all. The bird will enjoy picking off the bits of meat and cracking the bone to extract the marrow. The meat and marrow are valuable sources of protein.

I would never suggest feeding cooked chicken bones to cats or dogs, as splinters of bone frequently become lodged in the mouth, throat, or stomach. However, in nearly thirty years of avian veterinary practice I have never seen such a problem in parrots. These birds seem to crush the bone with their powerful beaks before swallowing it, and the tough lining of the gizzard completes the grinding process.

I am more reluctant to recommend pork or lamb chop or rib bones, purely because of the higher fat content, but I do have clients who give these items to their birds, with no obvious problem – as long as they are not fed to excess. As with many food items, parrots tend only to pick off the prime pieces, and would rarely in any case consume the whole bone.

Cooked fish is another valuable source of animal protein and its constituent amino acids, but raw fish is to be avoided, because it contains thiaminase, which will destroy the B-vitamin thiamine.

Dougal enjoying his regular cooked chicken bone. Note again the use of the foot to hold the food item, while the powerful beak cracks open and crushes the bone and the tongue extracts the nutritious marrow. Parrots are as much right- and left-footed as humans are right- and left-handed. This food is a valuable source of animal protein, calcium, and phosphorus, but should always be well-cooked – raw chicken could potentially carry infectious organisms such as Salmonella *or* E. coli.

up to a point: they do not have the enzyme lactase to digest milk sugar (lactose), but the worst that will happen to a bird fed a large quantity of milk is that it will have transient diarrhoea. As a first-aid source of calcium milk is invaluable, and a little hard cheese is enjoyed by most birds, as well as providing them with calcium and protein.

Calcium is required for bone formation, feather production, egg shell manufacture, and normal nerve and muscle function. Phosphorus is closely linked with calcium, and is also essential for bone formation. However, the ratio of calcium to phosphorus in the diet should be around 2:1. Phosphorus is contained in most foodstuffs, especially seeds and vegetables, while dry seeds are very low in calcium. Thus the conventional 'parrot seed mix' will have a Ca:P ratio of 1:10 or worse, resulting in serious calcium deficiency.

Iron is essential for haemoglobin, the oxygen-carrying pigment in red blood cells, and is found in fish and meat products, and wholemeal bread.

Many other minerals are required in smaller quantities, some so minute as to be termed trace elements. Magnesium is linked with calcium and phosphorus in bone formation, as well as enzyme activity. It is found in wheatgerm and sunflower. Copper is linked with iron in haemoglobin manufacture, and also in enzyme activity. It is present in meat, wheatgerm, nuts and oily seeds. Zinc is essential for the hormone insulin, and many enzyme activities. Selenium is required in digestive processes and hormone manufacture, as well as having an anti-oxidant effect. Manganese is essential for cartilage and bone growth, as well as reproductive function and egg-shell manu-facture. All three of these minerals are found in meats and fish, bone, wheatgerm and some oily seeds.

Iodine is an important element for proper func-tion of the thyroid gland, which in turn controls skin and feather quality as well as metabolic rate. It is present in wheatgerm and egg, as well as fish and seaweed products. Sodium, Chlorine and Potassium are additionally required for proper growth and development, but are present in plentiful amounts in most food items.

Problems caused by deficiency or excess of these vitamins and minerals will be discussed in more detail in Chapter 8.

Fibre and Grit

A certain amount of 'roughage' is essential in the diet to aid the digestive process. This is generally obtained in the form of cellulose fibres in fruits and vegetables. The addition of grit to the diet of parrots is contentious. It appears to be necessary for the smaller species that naturally consume a high-seed diet, such as budgerigars, cockatiels and grass parakeets. Larger parrots appear to manage perfectly well without it, and in fact may develop impaction problems if it *is* provided. The muscular gizzard, with its tough koilin lining, is more than capable of grinding up food items without the aid of grit.

If grit is used, it may be in the form of crushed oyster-shell, which gradually will be dissolved by stomach acid, giving up its calcium content to the bird in the process. Alternatively, it may be mineral grit – small pieces of stone, which is what parrots would naturally ingest in the wild. These are not digestible, but will gradually pass through the bird's digestive system to be voided, so will need regular replacement. It is not really necessary to leave a large dish of grit permanently in place in your bird's cage: access once a week is probably sufficient. Alternatively scatter a little across the floor, or sprinkle it over the food.

FEEDING YOUR PARROT A BALANCED DIET

So how can parrot-keepers best supply these essen-tial dietary constituents to their birds in a bal-anced, palatable form? It should now be clear that not only do different types of parrot require dif-ferent forms of food, but that nutritional require-ments will vary throughout the life of the bird, and that the standard seed-based diet is woefully inadequate. However, it will take many more generations of bird-keepers and a lot of education before we move away from using 'parrot mix' as the staple.

Seeds

Sunflower seeds and peanuts alone will lead to nutritional problems very quickly, and if you buy cheap, you will get rubbish. There is often no 'sell by' date on bags of loose seed mixes bought from the pet store, so one has no indication as to the age of the product. What nutrients are in the seed will deteriorate with time, and poor storage will hasten that decline. Add to that the possibility of rodent or insect contamination during storage, and such a cheap mix can be a positive danger to your birds.

Seeds taken for bird food are generally of poor quality anyway, having been classed as unfit for human consumption. The photograph [below] shows a selection of foreign material I retrieved from a sack of cheap, poorly cleaned parrot seed mix. It includes string, stone, wood, glass and mouldy peanuts.

Débris from the bottom of a cheap sack of seed mix, including string, blackened mouldy peanuts, stone, and wood. This indicates a mix that has been poorly cleaned and sieved, and obviously poses a risk to your parrots.

A proprietary parrot mix containing assorted seeds, but with the addition of dried fruits and small bread sticks. The sunflower seeds are still present, but have been 'hulled' to remove the seed husk and supply just the grey kernel.

If we accept that a seed mix is going to be used, then it should be varied and of good quality. Batches of seeds are cleaned by the producers, using sieves, magnets, air-blowers and the like. These techniques cost money, especially if repeated, so more expensive mixes will be of better quality.

Large macaws will need larger nuts added to the mix – these should be unsalted. Other commercial mixes are available that have additional dried fruits and small bread sticks added to the seeds and nuts to provide a more 'balanced' mix.

A seed mix containing some larger nuts as well as varied shapes and colours of formulated dry diet.

Roasted cashew nut kernels for human consumption. These are suitable for larger parrots, provided they are unsalted – excess salt is not good for parrots.

Fruits and Vegetables

In theory, it would be possible to balance your bird's diet by adding fresh fruits and vegetables to the seed mix. However, most birds – like young children – are selective eaters, and will shovel through the bowl to pick out their favourite items, dumping the rest on the floor. If you present most children with a table laid with a burger, broccoli, chips, banana, apple, cheese, chocolate, carrots, pizza, fresh tomatoes, crisps, ice cream and celery, you can imagine which items they will choose!

One way round this problem is to feed the 'healthy' items like fruits and vegetables separately in the morning, when the bird is hungry, and add the bowl of seed only at the end of the day, when the bird has previously had no choice but to eat the fresh food.

Vegetable products of all groups have high nutritive value for parrots. Items such as cucumber and lettuce may be enjoyed, but have high water content, so droppings will be very liquid after this sort of food. Harder, darker greens are preferable – kale, spinach, cabbage, broccoli, peas and beans are all palatable and enjoyed by most parrots.

It is often stated that oxalate in Brassica species (cabbages, etc.) will compete for digestive uptake with calcium. My clinical experience suggests that this is rarely a problem in practice, and that birds do obtain calcium as well as valuable vitamin A from such foods. Orange or yellow coloured vegetables such as carrots, maize (sweetcorn), yams, butternut squash and peppers are excellent sources of vitamin A and its carotenoid precursors.

Of the fruits, in general tropical fruits such as mango, papaya, bananas, and passion fruit have higher levels of 'good' nutrients (especially vitamins) than do temperate varieties like apples and pears. That is not to say that the latter are not good – parrots will enjoy them, and any fruit is better than none – but tropical fruits are even better.

The only fruit that must not be fed to parrots is avocado *(Persea* species). This is actively toxic to parrots, although many other bird species may consume it with impunity. So far as I am aware at the time of writing, the toxic principle still has not been identified, but both flesh and stone will harm parrots. Guatamalan and Nabal varieties appear to be more dangerous than Mexican strains.

Some parrots will quite happily have two adjacent bowls – one with fruits and vegetables, the

Chopped fruits and vegetables, including strawberry, celery, peas, grapes and carrot, added to a seed mix. However, the seeds are still mostly sunflower, with a few pine nuts, and the parrot is likely to pick out the sunflower seeds in preference to most other items.

Avocado pear – a luxury food item for humans, and safely consumed by some birds, but actively toxic to parrots. Both the stone and the flesh will cause gastro-enteritis, nervous signs, and even death in psittacine birds.

CASE STUDY: TOXIC AVOCADO

Avocado poisoning in parrots is not an old wives' tale – I have seen it happen on several occasions. A client of mine went away for a weekend, leaving her collection of six assorted parrots in the care of her daughter. The daughter dutifully came to the house and cleaned, fed and watered the birds.

Whilst there, she spotted a large, ripe avocado in the fruit bowl on the kitchen table. Thinking to give the parrots a special treat to cheer them up while Mum was away, she sliced the fruit and gave each bird a piece. Within hours several of the birds were looking miserable, showing signs of abdominal pain, hunched up and fluffed, with vomiting and diarrhoea.

I received a panicky phone call, and fortunately the history made the diagnosis easy, and supportive treatment was given to the birds. (There is no specific antidote, since the toxic principle is unknown.) Sadly, in spite of this, four birds died within twenty-four hours, and the remaining two that had consumed less of the fruit were extremely ill for several days.

Blue-fronted Amazon parrot (Amazona aestiva) *looking decidedly unwell. Its head is tucked under its wing, ignoring what is going on around it. Feathers are raised to maintain body heat, and the droppings are very liquid and abnormally coloured.*

other with seeds and nuts – and will eat successfully from both. For others it is better, as suggested, to feed the fruits and vegetables as a separate meal in the morning, with more chance that the parrot will be hungry and will take it if there is no seed on offer.

Beware of fruits in outdoor flights in a hot

Grey mould growth on ripe blackberries. Such mould contamination develops very quickly on ripe fruits in warm, humid conditions, and can be a serious risk to your parrots if eaten.

Wasps gathering on a slice of apple that had been 'spiked' on a perch for birds in an aviary. At best, a wasp sting is an unpleasant nuisance to a bird, and at worst it can kill them from anaphylactic shock.

summer. They will ferment, grow mould and deteriorate quickly, and will be a magnet for wasps. They should be offered in the cool of the morning and removed after a couple of hours.

A slice of apple fastened to the cage with a clothes peg, so that the parrot may nibble it at will. Some individuals will prefer food presented in this way, others prefer it chopped into smaller pieces.

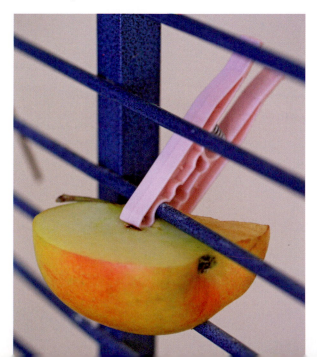

You will need to experiment with your bird. Some will prefer fruits and vegetables in large chunks that they can hold in their feet while biting pieces off. Others will eat from a portion that is fastened to the cage or aviary wire by means of a clip or wire holder. Yet others prefer the food to be chopped or diced into small fragments that they can pick up and swallow in one go.

When fruits are plentiful, free-living parrots naturally bite out a choice portion of fruit flesh and discard the rest of the fruit; or will bite through the flesh to get to the seeds at the core. Thus while they can be wasteful in their 'table manners', they are capable of opening fruits for themselves!

Many of my clients spend hours preparing fruits and vegetables in specific ways for their birds – more through their own preferences than the birds' – but with the result that the parrot gets used to eating the fruit in a certain way, and will not accept it if presented differently. One of my African grey patients will eat orange only if it is simply cut in half. She will then pick out the juice and flesh from the peel. Another bird – an Umbrella cockatoo – will take the same fruit only if it is peeled, divided into segments, and the white pith painstakingly removed by his owner!

Some birds will prefer cooked vegetables, others eat them raw. From a nutritional point of view, raw is obviously preferable, but a little gentle steaming, blanching, or microwaving will not seriously affect the nutritional content, and may make the item more palatable and enhance its flavour. I once had two African grey parrots – Eric and Cosworth. Eric would eat his carrots raw, while Cosworth would take them only if cooked. Again, see which your bird prefers. A little cooked vegetable is better than none at all.

Parrots are social feeders. They will fly out in family groups or large flocks in early morning and late afternoon to forage and feed together. In captivity, especially for indoor pet parrots, the human family is your bird's 'flock'. It will therefore be stimulated to eat when you do, and may want to join you. Many owners comment that their parrots eat most when the humans are having their evening meal. Those birds that have been allowed to do so may well make nuisances of themselves by coming to the table and taking

A selection of dried pulses – seeds of peas and beans. These may be fed to parrots in this state, but are less likely to be palatable.

The same pulses soaking in water.

After soaking for twenty-four hours, the pulses are softened and swollen. After thorough rinsing they may be fed to parrots in this state.

food from their owners' plates. This can be a good way of persuading the bird to try new food items, provided they are suitable (vegetables and salads), as he will want to taste what you are eating. All too often, however, it becomes a route to introduce pet parrots to human 'junk food' – pastry, chips and the like. Sugary fruit drinks are not advisable, and neither is alcohol!

Pulses

These are the fruiting bodies of leguminous vegetables – peas and beans in their many varieties. High in protein and several vitamins, pulses provide the increased intake of dietary protein needed to breed, lay eggs and rear chicks. Many bird-keepers feed these to their parrots, especially during the breeding season.

Pulses are purchased in a dried form, and before feeding they need to be soaked or cooked to make

The soaked pulses laid out on soaked tissue, which is kept moist for the next forty-eight hours.

After forty-eight hours soaking, the pulses have started to split and root shoots are showing. Germinating seeds like this have higher nutritive value, as vitamin and protein content increase.

them more palatable. A small batch should be thoroughly rinsed, then left to soak for twenty-four hours, with several changes of clean water during this period. After a final rinse, the softened soaked legumes may be fed to your birds. Many people take this a stage further and 'sprout' the pulses by laying the soaked beans on moist absorbent paper on a tray. After twenty-four to forty-eight hours, the seeds will split and begin to form shoots. After rinsing once again, these sprouted pulses will form an even better protein and vitamin-rich food source for your birds.

Other aviculturists advocate boiling their pulses first to remove toxins potentially present in some varieties of bean. The cooking process will also further soften the product, but will inevitably reduce some of its vitamin content. Again, the cooked pulses should be rinsed thoroughly before feeding to your parrots. Inadequate rinsing of both cooked and uncooked beans can lead to rapid contamination of the food with bacteria and fungi, with possible serious harm to your birds as a result.

A pulse diet is rich in both protein and some vitamins, but it is low in calcium so should not be fed as a sole food source. The diet will need the addition of calcium rich foods, or an avian-specific calcium supplement.

FORMULATED DIETS

From a nutritional standpoint, by far the better option is to feed your parrots on a properly balanced commercially formulated diet. The principle behind these diets is that quality ingredients are combined in appropriate proportions to provide a balance of essential nutrients, and then prepared by either extrusion or pelleting into conveniently-sized nuggets that the bird will consume. In theory your parrot will receive all its dietary requirements in the correct quantities; and there will be no waste as there are no seed husks or peel, and the bird cannot sort through to pick out its favourite items. In practice, this objective will depend on the quality of the raw materials used; the efficiency of the manufacturing process; the storage and transport of the finished product; and its palatability to and acceptance by your parrot.

The quality of the basic ingredients is paramount. One at least of the current manufacturers of formulated diets uses only certified organic products, with no colourings or preservatives. Other companies form the nuggets into a variety of strange shapes, and colour them with various

Commercial organically produced formulated mixes, in different granule size and fat content. 'High Potency' has a higher fat content, and is used for macaws and grey parrots, growing birds, initial encouragement to accept the product, and during breeding or moulting. 'Adult Lifetime' is used for maintenance in birds converted to the diet which are in stable, non-demanding adult phase. This brand is made entirely from organic ingredients, with no chemical additives, colourings, or preservatives.

Other formulated diets are shaped and coloured, but colourings used should be simple vegetable dyes, and not artificial chemicals.

pigments. The colouring is really to attract the human purchaser – the birds really do not seem to mind what colour it is as long as it tastes good! Colourants used should be simple vegetable dyes, and not the variety of artificial E-numbers used in so many human food products. These are known to cause hyperactivity problems in human children, and should be avoided in birds.

If no preservatives are used in the finished product, then storage, packaging, transport, and the manufacturing process are all important in order to avoid deterioration and rancidity. The extrusion process is performed at a high temperature, binding the ingredients and pasteurizing them to reduce bacterial contamination. The process also increases palatability and digestibility of the components. Pelleting is carried out at lower temperatures, with greater risk of bacterial contamination, more dust, and less palatability.

As understanding of birds' nutritional

Different grades of organic formulated diet. From top to bottom – coarse grind, fine grind, and mash – to suit different species.

A Blue and yellow and a Green-winged macaw showing bright eyes and immaculate, highly coloured plumage, as signs of good health and condition.

requirements increases, so the variety of formulated diets available also increases. They are now available in high-potency (higher fat content) for macaws and greys and breeding birds; lifetime formulae for maintenance; and with different granule size to suit different sizes of bird. This includes a mash for very small species or convalescing patients, and hand-rearing formulae for baby parrots.

It can be difficult to persuade a 'sunflower seed junkie' to take on a nutritionally superior formulated diet. There are many techniques suggested to aid the transition, and as each bird is different in its reaction, what will work for one may not be successful for another. Sometimes the 'cold turkey' method works. All other food is removed, and only the chosen formulated diet is offered. This may require hospitalization at a veterinary clinic for close monitoring of the bird and its bodyweight. Owners often will not persist with this technique for long enough, because parrots will hold out for many days until they get what they want. This can work for some individuals, and usually once converted they never look back.

In other cases a gradual introduction is successful. Nuggets can be mixed with the parrot's existing foods, or given in a separate bowl – some birds will select the food in this way. Alternatively, use the technique suggested for fruits and vegetables, giving the formulated food on its own in the morning, topping up with seed and nuts only in the evening. The bird will have had a good chance to sample the new food during the day. Warming the formula slightly will release oils and may improve its flavour. Adding a few drops of fruit juice may have the same effect. As mentioned earlier, parrots enjoy eating with the family, so passing the bird-formulated diet from a human plate may encourage it to take the new product.

An argument raised against formulated diets is that they are 'boring' for the bird. Variety and interest can be added to a pelleted diet in the form of fresh fruits and vegetables – up to 20 per cent of the total intake.

Food should not be used to provide stimulation. Parrots, in common with all animals, 'eat to live', they do not have the human feelings of anticipation, preparation, presentation, and socialization associated with eating. Agreed, they are intelligent and inquisitive, and in that respect food may be presented in different ways. Favoured items may be placed into hollow toys, small bags, or cardboard boxes for the parrot to explore and work out how to obtain them. But – giving food should not be used as the bird's sole source of amusement and occupation. Environmental enrichment has been discussed earlier in this book, and will be again. Parrots should have toys to play with, items to chew and destroy, and space and light to enrich their lives, not just endless food.

There is no doubt that parrots that take to a formulated diet with some fruit and vegetable do in the long term appear healthier and fitter, with better feather quality and colour than those on a seed-based diet. Breeding results are generally better as well.

SEASONAL VARIATION

It is natural for parrots to consume different foods as they come into season throughout the year, and captive parrots should be no exception. Whilst it is possible these days to obtain most foods

Rose hips – the fruits of wild dog roses. These are suitable for feeding to parrots, and are particularly rich in vitamin C.

throughout the year in supermarkets, locally-grown and harvested products are strictly seasonal, usually cheaper, and obviously environmentally friendly owing to minimal transportation. Why pay over the odds for specialist foods out of season? Use what comes in when it is available – freeze some if it is suitable – then move on to the next product. Parrots will happily consume fresh spring vegetables early in the year, moving on through the summer fruits and berries, to the autumn harvest of wild foods like rose hips, which are a valuable source of vitamin C and may be frozen. Pomegranates are a particular favourite with many parrots but naturally have a short season.

These birds' requirements are also very seasonal. When moulting out old feathers and growing new ones, their demand for calcium and protein will be high. The same requirements apply to young growing birds. Adults that are preparing to mate, lay eggs, and raise young will also need a higher nutritional plane, with extra protein, vitamins, and minerals – especially calcium. Birds recovering from stress, injury or illness may require extra carbohydrates and protein to replace weight loss and repair damaged tissues.

Outside of these times, normal maintenance requirements of parrots will be much reduced. This is particularly true of the less active, indoor pet parrot, which is kept warm and comfortable with a ready supply of food – so much so that in many cases these birds will become obese, especially if they are allowed to eat too much in the way of junk food.

UNDESIRABLE FOODS

We have already looked at junk foods as being unsuitable for parrots: pastry, chips, fried foods are as bad for birds in excess as they are for humans. Foods that are high in carbohydrate and fat but low in protein, such as sunflower seeds, will cause the bird to overeat in order to acquire sufficient protein, as explained above. However, wheatgerm appears frequently in the list of products containing several essential vitamins and minerals, so wholemeal bread or toast is perfectly suitable to supply these items.

However, this is all a matter of degree: too much of the bad items and not enough of the good. To my mind there are just three absolutely forbidden foods for parrots:

The first is *avocado*, which as we have already found is toxic to parrots.

The second is *salted food*: there is sufficient salt for parrots' needs contained within their foods, without adding to it; excess salt will lead to kidney damage, so salted crisps or nuts should never be given.

The third is *chocolate*: theobromines and theophylline are known to be actively poisonous to dogs, and will over-stimulate birds' hearts, making them at least hyper-active and at worst causing heart failure.

SPECIALIST DIETS

Large macaws like the hyacinthine do need a higher fat intake than most other parrot species. They will enjoy walnuts and brazil nuts, but their favourites are palm nuts.

Fig parrots (*Opopsitta* and *Psittaculirostris* spp.) have a higher than average requirement for vitamin K. It is believed that these birds have lost the ability to absorb plant-derived vitamin K, and depend on bacterial formation of this vitamin in the gut, and

One of the Red lory group showing the brush-tipped tongue for gathering pollen and nectar.

they obtain these bacteria from termites, in whose mounds they often nest.

Lories and lorikeets, as well as other brush-tongued species such as hanging parrots and swift parakeets, feed naturally on nectar and pollen. Keepers of these birds originally made their own 'nectar mixes' from honey, fruit juices and sponge cake. Now there are several proprietary brands of lory nectar available, and these are given along with fresh fruits. Keeping these birds tends still to be a specialist enthusiast and labour-intensive hobby, however. They produce very messy sticky droppings, and food has to be changed several times a day; the nectar will ferment and spoil in hot weather, and may freeze in cold weather.

SUPPLEMENTS

It should now be clear that parrots have complex and varied feeding requirements. Those requirements will vary according to species, age, sex, breeding and moulting cycles, environmental temperature, and time of year. In theory birds fed a formulated diet with fresh vegetables and fruit should need no additions to their diet, but most parrots given seed-based foods will be fitter and healthier if they are given vitamin and mineral supplements to compensate for any inherent imbalance, as well as their natural inclination to feed selectively. Such supplements should be avian-specific, rather than using products intended for cats and dogs.

Water-soluble products tend to be less stable than powdered equivalents, to deteriorate quickly in drinking water and not to be consumed in sufficient quantity, as parrots generally drink little. Powdered supplements may be added to food, but this should be either moist sticky food that is readily consumed by the bird, such as fruit, or items that may be moistened, like egg-biscuit or wholemeal bred. Simply sprinkling the powder over dry seed will be pointless, since the powder will drop to the bottom of the food bowl.

The type of supplement chosen may be varied with specific needs throughout the year, following the birds' changing requirements for proteins, vitamins and minerals as they breed, lay eggs, and moult feathers.

Finally, if you have obtained a bird that has been hand-reared, it will be accustomed to taking moist food from a spoon or syringe. It is worth continuing to offer your pet small amounts of bird-safe soft foods like live yogurt or fruit and cereal-based baby foods on an occasional basis. This is not for any 'bonding' reason, but to make it easier to administer any oral medications that may be required in the future. It is so much easier to give parrots drugs disguised in a familiar treat in this way than it will be to try to syringe-dose the medicine to an unwilling, struggling patient!

Young African grey parrot being spoon-fed with a juvenile feeding formula via shaped teaspoon. Birds that are accustomed to feeding in this way will readily take supplements or medications added to formula.

CHAPTER 7

Breeding Parrots

If you keep a budgerigar, cockatiel or small parrot for a while, you may decide to add to your collection, and even try to breed them. Or you may have set out to establish a breeding collection when you started parrot-keeping. Whatever led you to deciding to breed, you need to go about it the right way in order to have any success.

All mature female animals produce eggs on a regular cycle. Creatures like fish and amphibians have their eggs fertilized outside the body by the male, who has been following her closely, waiting for the moment. Birds, reptiles, and a few egg-laying mammals mate, with the male's sperm fertilizing the eggs *inside* the female before they are laid. The fertilized egg then produces an embryo that grows and develops inside the egg, outside the mother's body. The embryo is kept warm during its development either by brooding performed by the parents, or by warmth generated by burying the eggs in soil or vegetable matter. The majority of mammals, of course, plus a few reptiles and fish, will retained the fertilized eggs to develop inside the parent. When the embryos reach a suitable stage of development, the animal will give birth to live young.

Many clients are surprised, and even a little upset, when their single pet bird suddenly produces an egg. Many an African grey parrot called Charlie or Fred has startled its owner by laying an egg at the age of fifteen or twenty. If you keep a hen cockatiel, it is almost impossible to stop her laying eggs – these birds are almost as prolific as chickens. 'But she has no male bird with her!' is the usual reaction. A female does not need the presence of a male to produce an egg – that is a natural and regular process. Domestic chickens are bred to produce eggs on a massive scale and on an almost daily basis. The sole purpose of the male is to fertilize that egg, but his absence won't stop the hen producing one.

COCKS AND HENS

Thus a single pet female parrot may produce the occasional egg. But if you want to breed parrots properly, you will obviously need at least one mature pair of male and female specimens of the same species. Breeding parrots is not like breeding cats and dogs. You cannot simply take a hen bird off to a 'stud cock' in the way that bitches or queens in season are taken to mate with selected stud dogs or tom cats. These birds generally require a prolonged courtship and bonding period – which can take several years – before they will breed successfully.

Many important factors are involved in the successful breeding of parrots. The birds should be of similar age, and at least approaching sexual maturity. They should be healthy. I have covered the selection of birds in earlier chapters, and it may be worthwhile having screening tests for infectious diseases, such as PBFD (psittacine beak and feather disease), PDD (proventricular dilatation disease) or Chlamydiosis, before introducing new birds to your collection.

Many people have suggested that ex-pet or captive-bred birds are unsuitable for breeding. While this may be true with the odd individual that is heavily imprinted on humans, as a general rule the idea has been disproved on many occasions. It is therefore not necessary to use only wild-caught parrots for breeding.

BAD FOR BUSINESS

In the late 1980s and early 1990s in the UK, many parrot-keepers decided they could make easy money by setting up a breeding colony of parrots. At that time African grey parrots *(Psittacus erithacus)* were still being imported from the wild in large numbers and were comparatively cheap, while hand-reared (HR) baby greys were selling in pet stores at a premium. The thinking was to buy perhaps ten pairs of greys from the importer and set them up in an aviary complex. Each pair would produce three or more chicks a year that could be sold for several hundred pounds each, and *voilà* – fortune made!

In practice, few people achieved this objective. Birds died; they didn't lay eggs or if they did the eggs didn't hatch; those chicks that did hatch died young, and certainly were not produced in large numbers each year. Many owners were impatient if their parrots did not breed within the first twelve months, so partners were swapped or the birds were sold on to other keepers. Most became disillusioned with the whole idea, and eventually abandoned parrot-breeding. Those breeders that remain are those that have had the patience and determination to do the job properly and get the best out of their birds.

Juvenile African grey parrot showing the bright shiny beak and grey iris in the eye typical of the young bird. (See also page 38.)

Sex Determination

It is not always easy to tell the sex of a parrot. I mentioned briefly in Chapter 1 that those birds in which there *is* an obvious difference between male and female are known as dimorphic (two forms). In game-birds and most waterfowl the differences are very marked, and especially in the breeding season males have flamboyant plumage while the hens are generally well camouflaged in speckled brown. The only parrot with this significant difference is the Eclectus, in which the feather colouring is so remarkably different that these birds were once thought to be different species. The hen birds are primarily red, with some blue and purple, while the cock birds are mostly green. These feather colours are visible as soon as feathers grow, so the chicks may be sexed in the nest. In other species plumage differences are more subtle, and generally evident only in the adult bird, such as the dark coloured neck feathering of the cock ring-necked parakeet, not present in juveniles and hens; or the even more obvious neck ring of its cousin the Alexandrine parakeet.

It is possible – because birds can visualize ultraviolet wavelengths of light – that plumage differences undetectable to the human eye are seen by birds. Other sexually dimorphic parrots have different features. In most budgerigars the cere, the fleshy area above the beak containing the nostrils, is blue in the adult male and brown

Female Eclectus parrot with red, blue and mauve feathers typical of her sex. She also has a black beak. The cock bird has green and red feathers, with a yellow/orange beak, as can be seen in the photograph on page 28.

in the female. Some white and yellow budgies will have a neutral mauve cere, and abnormal hormone levels may alter the normal colour. Abnormal hormones released from testicular tumours in the male may turn his blue cere brown, while the reverse may occur in hen birds with ovarian cysts or tumours.

In most white cockatoos the iris colour in the eye is different in adult birds, being reddish-brown in the hen and dark brown/black in the cock bird. Juvenile cockatoos have a neutral hazel colour. Shades of colour are variable, and some very dark brown eyes are seen in hens, but rarely are light brown eyes found in cocks.

There may be more subtle differences, such as the head size and beak shape mentioned in Chapter 3. The adult cock African grey parrot and some Amazons have broad, flat heads, with a 'Roman-nose' profile. Hen birds have narrower, rounder heads, with beaks curving on a separate radius to the crown of the head.

Many of the species we deal with, however, have no visible differences between the sexes. These are known as monomorphic (one form), and this applies particularly to many of the parrot family. Such visibly identical cocks and hens will require scientific tests to confirm their sex.

Adult Umbrella cockatoo (Cacatua alba) *showing the reddish-brown iris, indicating that she is a hen bird.*

Adult male Goffin's cockatoo (Cacatua goffini) *with a dark brown, almost black iris.*

CASE STUDY: BOY OR GIRL?

As always, there are exceptions to every rule. Arthur was a Greater sulphur-crested cockatoo *(Cacatua galerita)* with very dark eyes, a large heavy beak, and general male behaviour. He preferred human females to men, and he performed masturbatory activity on his perch.

Over many months he developed a progressive ventral hernia of the body wall, which eventually required surgical repair. When we opened the hernial sac, it was a big surprise to find a rudimentary oviduct containing several small egg-shaped masses! This bird appeared to be a hermaphrodite, with the physical appearance of a male, but with internal organs partially female. There were two gonads – one like a normal testis, but the other nodular and irregularly shaped.

The exception that proves the rule: Arthur, a Greater sulphur-crested cockatoo (Cacatua galerita), with very dark eyes, suggesting that he is a male.

A close-up of Arthur's eye, showing the very dark iris.

Arthur being anaesthetized ready for surgery to investigate and repair the ventral hernia.

Close-up of the swollen hernia, with abraded skin surface.

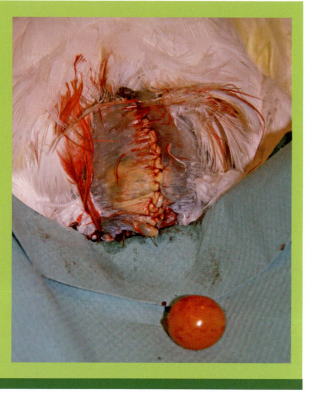

The repaired hernia, with one of the small egg-yolks removed from within the sac.

The first of these tests is chromosomal karyo-typing (DNA sexing). This is a simple technique involving the sampling of a small drop of blood or a blood feather that is sent away to a specialist laboratory. Results are obtained in about one week, and the owner will have the confirmation of the bird's gender. However, this test will just give that simple 'cock or hen' answer. If you seriously want to breed parrots successfully, the alternative technique of sex determination by endoscopy (so-called surgical sexing) will prove more beneficial.

Endoscopy sexing has some disadvantages. It is an invasive, minor surgical technique in which a small probe attached to a fibre-optic light source is inserted through the body wall to visualize the

Broad flat head of the adult cock African grey parrot. In profile, the curve of the forehead flows smoothly into that of the beak.

Close-up of the head of an adult Orange-winged Amazon showing variation in the distribution of yellow and blue, plus the orange-brown iris of the adult bird. This male bird has the similar heavy profile of the cock African grey, as shown on pages 60 and 129.

The more delicate form of the adult hen Grey parrot. The crown is narrower and rounder, while there is a 'stop' between the curve of the skull and that of the beak.

ovary or testes. While the probe may be as small as 1.9mm in diameter, there is still an obvious size limitation to the species of bird that will take this procedure. I am not comfortable sexing birds smaller than a cockatiel by this method. All the following information will therefore apply only to birds this size and larger. The operation requires a general anaesthetic, and this carries a small risk to the patient, as it does with any animal. Modern

anaesthetic agents, used by an experienced veterinarian, have minimized this risk factor, but it does still exist.

All parrots have internal gonads – both the testes of the male and the single left ovary of the female are situated in the abdominal cavity close to the kidneys. The organs will vary considerably in size according to the age of the bird and the stage of its breeding cycle. In juvenile birds the immature

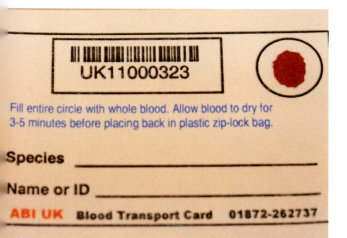

One method of submitting a sample for DNA analysis: a drop of blood from the bird is placed within the circle on the absorbent card, and despatched to the laboratory once dry.

Endoscopic sexing of a Green-winged macaw (Ara chloroptera). The bird is anaesthetized using gas via a face-mask, and the endoscope is inserted through the left flank of the bird to visualize the gonad(s).

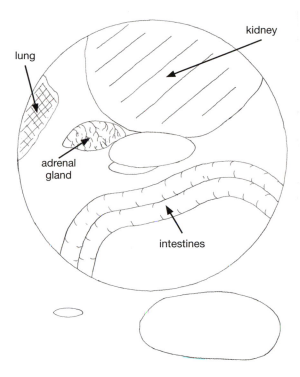

Diagrammatic representation of the endoscopic view inside an adult male bird. The veterinarian will see part of the lung at top left, loops of intestine or stomach in the lower right quadrant, and a large part of the anterior pole of the left kidney in the upper quadrant. Just below and forward of the kidney is the adrenal gland, with visible blood vessels. Over this gland is the smooth, oval left testis of this cock bird, with the right testis visible behind it. Testes of this size in relation to the other organs would indicate an adult male not in breeding phase. The testis of a juvenile bird would appear about the size of the subsidiary diagram to the lower left (outside the circle) while in a bird in full breeding condition the testis would enlarge to that shown at the lower right (outside the circle).

testes and ovary are very small and indistinct, so endoscopy examination will not be able to determine the sex of very young birds. This lower age limit is about twelve weeks for a bird the size of an average Amazon or African grey parrot. DNA sexing, on the other hand, can be performed on samples taken from babies still in the nest.

Skill and experience are required to find and correctly identify the gonads. Generally they are cream in colour, but in some species they may be grey. I have seen one individual male with one

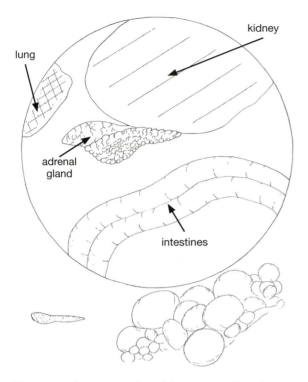

Diagrammatic representation of the corresponding view inside an adult female bird. The same landmarks of lung, kidney, and intestines are seen, but in this case overlying the adrenal gland is the irregularly shaped ovary with a nodular surface. In a young adult hen, this would have the appearance of semolina or frog-spawn. Again, the relative size of the ovary in a juvenile bird is shown at lower left, so it is clear that at this age (less than twelve weeks) it would be easy to confuse testis with ovary. The actively cycling ovary would appear as at lower right, with large ripening follicles.

testis cream and the other grey, and another bird where just one half of one testis was grey, with the other half cream.

Because the gonads are closely applied to the kidneys and adrenal glands, and are also near to the lungs and stomach, it is possible to seriously damage these vital organs, so once again care and experience are required. As the birds mature, the gonads will develop and enlarge, so it is possible to advise the owner whether or not the parrot is mature enough to breed. There will be fluctuation at different stages of the breeding cycle: inactive resting testes like those in the photograph will enlarge as much as tenfold, reaching the size of

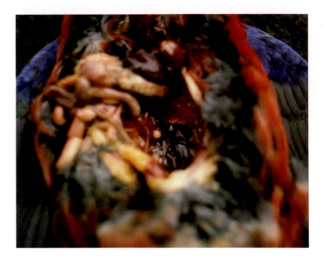

Post-mortem view of a male bird with its left testis pigmented grey, while the right is the more usual cream/pink.

the bird's heart when in full breeding condition. In the hen bird, ripening follicles will reach a large size just before egg laying. It is also possible to tell if the hen has laid eggs previously, by the presence of scarring from evacuated follicles in the ovary. Abnormalities of the testes will be visible, and may explain why a cock bird is not fertilizing eggs produced by his mate.

Large mature testes in an adult cock in breeding condition. They are smooth, oval, creamy pink, and closely attached to the anterior lobes of the kidneys.

RIGHT: *Post-mortem view of a young adult hen bird with a fungal growth in the thoracic air sac that was the cause of its demise. The young adult (but inactive) ovary is visible as a cream, vaguely triangular organ with a nodular surface, between the lung and the anterior lobe of the kidney.*

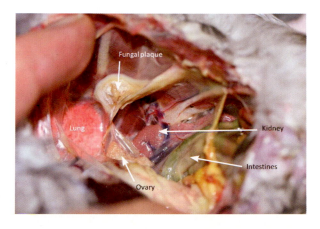

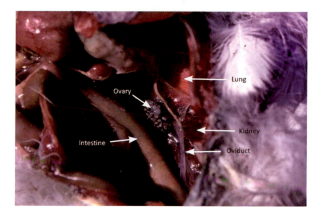

ABOVE: *Another post-mortem view of a white cockatoo, showing a mature ovary, in this case pigmented grey.*

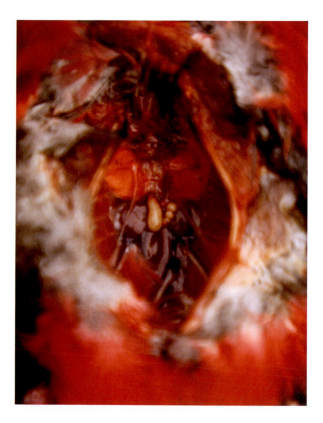

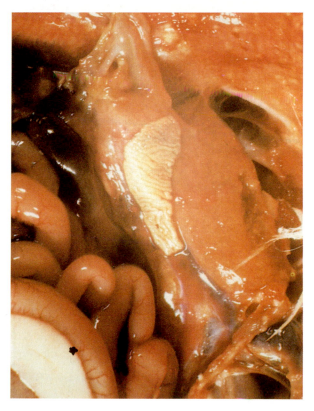

ABOVE: *Loops of bowel lower left, immature ovary centre, an amorphous, slightly textured, cream-coloured organ.*

LEFT: *Post-mortem view of an adult male bird with a normal right testis, but a deformed left organ showing several constrictions. The pink lungs are visible at the top of the picture, with the dark brown kidneys under and below the testes.*

Stainless-steel split ring applied by a veterinary surgeon following endoscopic sexing of the parrot, carrying the vet's initials plus a unique number.

Jendaya conure (Aratinga jandaya) *bearing two rings. Its left leg has a closed ring placed by the breeder when it was a chick; the right leg has a split ring secured with a rivet. The gold colour denotes a hen bird: a cock bird would be given a black ring.*

It is also possible at the time of the endoscopy to visualize other organs like the kidney, lung, air sacs, and parts of the digestive tract, thereby providing further information as to the health status of the parrot. Thus we may inform the owner immediately not only the sex of the bird, but also whether

Sexing ring in coloured aluminium, again carrying veterinarian's initials, but in this case blue was used for male, and red for female. Over the years, this ring, being a little tight and wide for this bird's leg, has rubbed on the limb and produced a callus.

it is mature enough to breed, or old and past it; in breeding condition or quiescent; and diseased or otherwise internally damaged. This is obviously more valuable information than the simple 'male/female' answer of the DNA technique, especially when trying to investigate a fertility problem.

Birds that have been endoscopically sexed by an experienced avian veterinarian are then identified with a leg ring (band) with unique lettering and numbering. Most are stainless steel, bearing the initials of the operative, followed by a number. Some veterinarians use numbered rings, secured with a rivet and made of gold coloured metal for the female and black for the male, thus showing a visible distinction. The stainless steel rings by convention are placed on the bird's right leg if it is a cock, and the left leg if it is a hen. The hen has a single ovary, and this is on the left side of her body, hence the endoscopy site is through the left flank, so the ring is placed on her left leg. Or – 'the male is always right!'

Compatibility

Having found your male and female birds, they have to be introduced! Sometimes it is love at first sight, usually it takes a little longer – all birds

Birds that have been together for several seasons without producing eggs should be investigated endoscopically to confirm that you have a true pair, and that they are healthy and in breeding condition. If diet and housing are good, and the birds are sound, then you may try moving the nest box, changing the aviary, or supplying the birds with alternative partners. Most parrots are very sensitive to their surroundings when breeding, and will be prevented from so doing by anything from prowling predators or vermin, environmental disturbances, to birds in neighbouring flights or nest boxes poorly sited. According to the direction of prevailing winds, the amount of shelter provided, and the exposure to sunlight, nesting areas can become very hot or too cold. Keepers may have to modify the birds' circumstances several times over a number of seasons before they will breed successfully. There is always the odd exception however.

A bonded pair of Blue and yellow macaws (Ara ararauna) *mutually preening. This activity is an important part of the behaviour of breeding birds. (Photo: Jan Hooimeijer)*

are different. Many aviculturists will place birds together in random pairs and have some degree of success, but it is not really too surprising to find that not every pair will breed successfully.

The ideal situation would be to have a communal flight in which all the eligible birds could be placed, outside their breeding season. Observation of their behaviour will show those birds that respond to each other and spend time sitting together and mutually preening. These naturally bonding pairs should then be separated off into the breeding quarters.

CASE STUDY
DEVOTED COUPLE

I once had a client who purchased a pair of Blue and yellow macaws from a fellow breeder. His timing was unfortunate however, as when he went to collect the birds, he found they were in their nest box with two eggs.

He had travelled a long way, and the seller desperately wanted to get rid of them, so the purchaser sealed the nest box with birds and eggs inside, and strapped the box to the back of his motorcycle! After a long and noisy journey home, the nest box was transferred to its new position in the waiting flight, and the birds were given food and water.

To everyone's surprise and delight the macaws contentedly continued to incubate their eggs. The eggs later hatched, and two chicks were raised successfully. Most other parrots would quickly have abandoned their eggs in these circumstances, and probably not bred again for a year or two, but not these two!

Purpose-built block containing breeding birds. There are no outside flights; windows are double-glazed; ventilation is positive-pressure, with temperature and humidity controlled; lighting is timer-controlled and on dimmers.

NEST BOX

I have outlined in an earlier chapter the housing options for your parrots. You may choose to have a single pair in a large indoor aviary; or several pairs in a birdroom, converted garage or stable; or purpose-built flights with indoor quarters.

The nest box is usually sited in an indoor or sheltered section, under cover. Nest box construction will vary with the species of bird being bred. It may be made of plywood for budgerigars or small parakeets, through larger boxes with thicker plywood, up to wooden or plastic barrels or even hollowed-out tree trunks for larger cockatoos and macaws.

There should be an entry hole near the top of the box to allow the parrots access to the interior. The size of the opening should correspond to the shoulder-width of the species concerned. There should be some form of perching mounted below this hole, or close to it. Most boxes are mounted vertically, but some species prefer horizontal or diagonally mounted boxes. Tunnel nesters like Patagonian conures *(Cyanoliseus patagonus)* will certainly prefer a long, horizontal box.

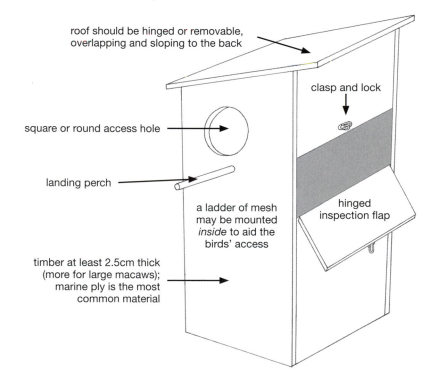

roof should be hinged or removable, overlapping and sloping to the back

clasp and lock

square or round access hole

landing perch

a ladder of mesh may be mounted *inside* to aid the birds' access

hinged inspection flap

timber at least 2.5cm thick (more for large macaws); marine ply is the most common material

Representation of a standard vertical parrot nest box, showing entrance hole with access perch for the bird, plus inspection flap for the breeder. NB: do not fix the box with enough space between its top and the roof of the aviary to allow either the birds or vermin to sit on top.

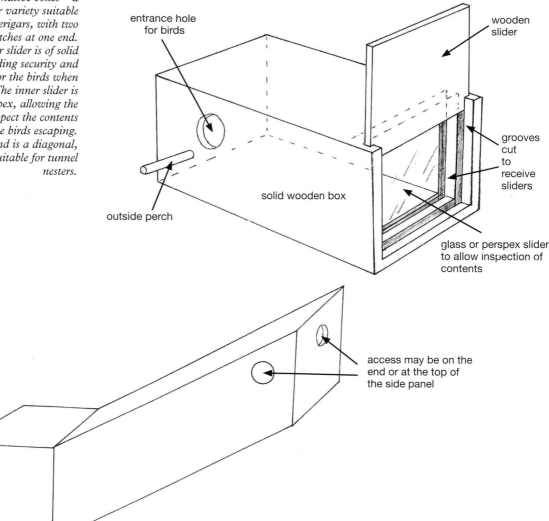

Alternative boxes – a smaller variety suitable for budgerigars, with two sliding hatches at one end. The outer slider is of solid wood, providing security and darkness for the birds when closed. The inner slider is glass or perspex, allowing the breeder to inspect the contents without the birds escaping. The second is a diagonal, long box suitable for tunnel nesters.

entrance hole for birds

wooden slider

grooves cut to receive sliders

solid wooden box

outside perch

glass or perspex slider to allow inspection of contents

access may be on the end or at the top of the side panel

Usually there is an inspection hatch on the opposite side of the box, accessible by the aviculturist from outside the cage or aviary. This will allow examination of the nest and eggs, and removal of chicks for ringing or hand-rearing, with minimal disturbance to the parents. Get your birds accustomed to such interference before the breeding season, so that they accept your presence and observation. Otherwise they may abandon the

Patagonian conure Buzz (Cyanoliseus patagonus). In the wild, these birds nest in tunnels in sandy banks or cliffs.

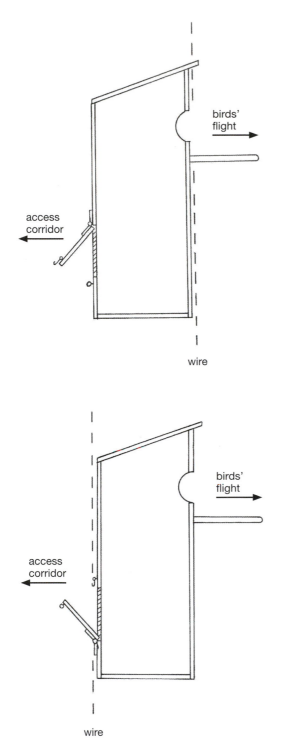

Nest boxes may be mounted inside or outside the aviary, either way allowing the breeder access via the inspection hatch.

nest, break the eggs, or kill the chicks if the interference is sudden and unexpected. Tap on the box, or whistle and call out as you approach to give the birds warning. Parrots will rapidly become accustomed to regular noise like trains or aeroplanes and noisy children, but unexpected loud commotion will seriously disturb nesting birds. Retrieving eggs from aggressive birds may necessitate some form of arm shield.

Adjacent flights should be double-wired or even have solid panelled sides, as described in Chapter 4, to avoid jealousy or territorial disputes with neighbouring pairs of birds.

Apart from Quaker parakeets (*see* Chapters 1 and 3), most parrots are hole dwellers, and will spend some time carving out the nest chamber from an old tree or other natural cavity. This is part of the developmental process of breeding behaviour, and along with finding and courting a mate and foraging for food, makes up a large part of the cock bird's activities at the start of the breeding season.

Therefore filling the nest box with old off-cuts of wood, or even partially blocking the entrance hole with wood, will give the birds work in chewing the material to line the nest. The provision of ready-made nest material of peat or sawdust – apart from the risk of fungal infections from the former – bypasses this essential nest-building stage. It is, however, helpful to provide a 'ladder' of wire mesh

DOMESTIC VIOLENCE

Male cockatoos particularly can be very aggressive when breeding, and there have been many instances where cock birds have savagely attacked their hens, resulting in major damage to head and beak, or even death. (Inexperienced parents may do the same to their chicks, especially if disturbed or if the chick behaves abnormally.) My opinion is that a large part of this 'domestic violence' is the result of a lack of the normal courtship procedure.

(with sharp edges cut or filed off) fixed inside the box and leading up to the entrance hole. This will aid entry and exit for the parents, and ease the chicks' exploration of the outside world when they are old enough.

In the wild, the cock bird will spend a lot of time and energy in finding and defending a suitable nest site; finding and courting a female; coaxing her to the nest; foraging for food gifts for her; as well as modelling and shaping the nest hole with the hen. All of this effort both absorbs his energy, and allows time for the hen to develop into full breeding receptivity.

In captivity, we provide two birds with a safe and secure home; a fully-furnished and ready-made nest box; and plenty of food *ad lib* so no foraging is required. Therefore the cock bird has no work to do and just wants to get on with the mating. The hen has not been suitably wooed, and is not ready for his advances, so the frustrated cock bird attacks her. Some keepers advocate clipping the wings of the cock bird, or fitting an escape hatch for the hen in the bottom of the nest box, so that the male cannot chase and corner the female.

It is better to try to encourage as far as possible the natural courtship activity, by letting the birds finish off the nest box to their satisfaction. Make them work for their food – feed only at selected times, and conceal items in boxes or toys. Increase the nutritional quality of the food leading up to the breeding season, as described below.

It is also likely that neighbouring birds or human interference may frustrate the cock bird. He will then attack the only animal he can reach – his unfortunate hen. It is therefore important to offer seclusion and privacy to breeding birds. Remember that breeding adult parrots will become aggressive and territorial at this time, in defence of their nest and young, so respect their needs.

BREEDING DIETS

Free-living parrots have a breeding season that coincides with peak availability of food. In temperate regions especially, outside of this season food is often scarce or of poor quality, allowing 'maintenance rations' only. As environmental temperatures rise, or rainfall encourages plant growth, then the birds will come into breeding condition, start to pair off, and hunt for nest sites. Outside of the tropics, increasing hours of daylight (photoperiod) will also have an influence. This natural cycle may be mimicked with captive parrots by feeding maintenance rations throughout rest of the year, and increasing the photoperiod as the breeding season approaches. This will be achieved naturally with outdoor birds in temperate zones, as spring and summer arrive. Indoor birds may be moved outside, or by using timer-controlled artificial lighting.

The food offered should have more and fresher ingredients, with an increase in protein and calcium content. These items are necessary for egg production and shell formation, and should be continued after chicks hatch to ensure healthy growth and development of the youngsters. Parent birds may benefit from the availability of soft foods to feed their chicks. These include soaked or sprouted pulses, soaked crushed or rolled oats or ground rice, or soaked egg food (dried egg with crushed biscuit). Fresh clean water should always be available to your birds, but it is doubly important at this time that the bowls are kept clean, uncontaminated, and regularly refreshed.

INCUBATION AND HAND-REARING

As a general rule parrot parents do a far better job of incubating eggs and rearing their chicks than do human carers. However, there may be times when it is necessary to take eggs for incubation or chicks for artificial rearing.

It has in the past been common practice for aviculturists to take eggs from breeding pairs, thereby encouraging the birds to produce another clutch and thus increasing productivity. This is a selfish, pecuniary attitude on the part of the bird-keeper, and in the long term will only weaken the hen and shorten her productive life. All the follicles a hen bird will ever have in her lifetime are present in the ovary from the beginning; they do not multiply in number, they simply grow in size. So whilst there are plenty of eggs, taking two or even three clutches from the hen in each breeding season will shorten her potential reproductive span by 50–60 per cent.

Another reason that was put forward for incubating eggs or hand-rearing chicks was to produce tame, manageable birds for the pet market. It is now clear after several decades of such practice that this objective has not been that successful. Incubation of eggs requires specialized equipment and tightly controlled conditions (*see* below). The death rate of embryos lost in the eggs is generally higher than that encountered in natural incubation. Successful hatching of live chicks can be problematic – usually as a result of too much interference made too soon by the breeder.

The hand-rearing of chicks is a time-consuming and demanding process, as many aviculturists will testify. Getting the quantity, consistency, temperature, nutritional balance, and feeding frequency of an appropriate mix is difficult. Many breeders over the years have mixed their own formulae with varying degrees of success, and there are now commercial products available to make the job easier. However, in my experience, the majority of chicks reared straight from the egg by humans are still not as robust and healthy as those fed by their parents. The only exception to this would be if the parents

A pair of Citron-crested cockatoo chicks taken for hand-rearing, as their parents rejected them.

themselves are given poor-quality food, but in that case it is hardly likely that the aviculturist will feed the chicks any better.

All animals that raise their own young pass on protective antibodies in the first few days of life. These antibodies will protect the youngster against infectious agents to which the parent is already immune. In mammals this is achieved via the milk – the colostrum produced in the first few days after birth is rich in such important agents. Parrots feed their chicks by regurgitating food that has been broken up and softened in the crop and proventriculus. This food is mixed with protein-rich secretions from the lining of the upper digestive tract, and these secretions contain the essential antibodies to give the chick a strong head start.

Obviously, such a system is not available to chicks hand-reared from day one, so they tend to be less robust and more likely to succumb to infection. Thus there is an argument for allowing the parents to feed the chick(s) for the initial week at least, and then to take the babies to 'finish off' by hand-feeding.

CASE STUDY
HAND-REARED VS WILD-CAUGHT

The argument that hand-reared baby parrots make better pets certainly does not hold water. Most youngsters, if given human contact and handling at weaning, will become tame and used to people very quickly.

I have a client with two African grey parrots. One was originally a wild-caught, imported young bird, and is now the tamest, most manageable pet you could ever wish for. His second bird was hand-raised by a breeder from hatching and was initially fine, but now has become a growler and screecher when approached, and will not tolerate any handling at all.

Every parrot is an individual, and its behaviour will be determined partly by its genetic makeup, and partly by its environment and upbringing.

Commercial 'production-line' for parrot chicks, showing several hatchers, plus plastic bins to hold the older chicks.

Many hand-fed baby parrots were produced in a 'production-line', with minimal human contact at feeding time only, and then tipped out into the pet market with absolutely no social skills – either avian or human! The problems raised in these birds as they mature will be discussed in further detail in Chapter 10.

So – incubation and hand-rearing of parrots for commercial gain and increased productivity for pet birds is to be discouraged, and is not in the best interests of the parrots we purport to be caring for. However, adult parrots may suffer illness or accident, leading to their eggs being abandoned. Some inexperienced parents may persistently break or eat their eggs. In these cases, eggs may be taken for incubation; although it is wise in the latter example not to take all the eggs – otherwise the adults will never learn to be good parents.

Abandoned eggs are easy to collect, but if you have to take eggs from an active pair, then be aware that some species – notably Amazons and some macaws – can be very protective of their nest boxes. I have already described above the provision of an access flap to the nest box, allowing the aviculturist access from the outside. The birds may be distracted or attracted into the flight by a colleague or treat, then you may have a drop-down door that you can close over the birds' entrance to the nesting area. Otherwise you can use a well-padded sleeve over your arm, or a length of plastic

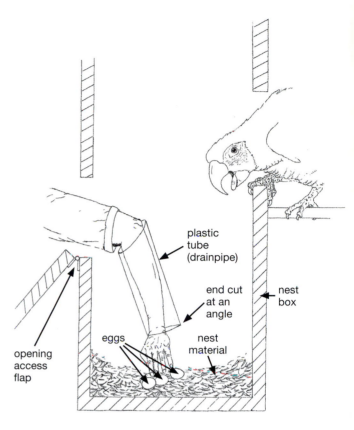

Collecting eggs may require a protective sleeve (in this case cut from plastic drainpipe).

pipe cut at an angle to protect your hand while collecting the eggs.

Using an Incubator

Having retrieved the eggs, they need to be placed in an incubator. This is essentially a box that is heated, to safely contain the eggs until they hatch. There are several types on the market, and several books dedicated in detail to their use. The size required will depend upon how many eggs you plan to incubate. They run most efficiently when well-filled, so do not buy a huge machine if you have only two or three eggs to incubate.

The important thing is to anticipate, and have the machinery set up and stabilized well before you put the eggs in. Ideally, the incubator should be set up in a dedicated room that is quiet, easily cleaned, and of a stable temperature. Wildly fluctuating

Two clutches of eggs marked and collected, waiting to be placed in the incubator so that they all hatch at about the same time.

natural state, most parrots lay eggs on alternate days, and will not settle to incubate properly until the clutch is complete. This means that all the eggs should hatch at around the same time. If eggs are collected for artificial incubation once the whole clutch has been produced, then replicating this process should be no problem. However, if they are collected individually as soon as they are laid (from a known egg-eater or egg-breaker perhaps), then the first few eggs may be stored in a tray in the incubation room until the clutch is complete. Each egg should be marked with the laying date and a number.

ambient temperature (in a kitchen or conservatory, for example) will have the incubator struggling to maintain a steady optimum level for the eggs. Both temperature and humidity are critical for successful hatching, and incubators will have thermostatically-controlled heating elements, as well as water reservoirs and systems to adjust humidity. Average temperatures required are around 37°C, with humidity at this stage of about 40 per cent.

In nature, the parent birds will regularly turn their eggs, moving those on the outside of a large clutch to the centre of the group, and vice versa, so that each egg is kept within an even range of temperature and humidity. This procedure is mimicked in the incubator by a system of rollers attached to a timed motor, which will rotate the eggs at pre-determined intervals. Such action will prevent the embryo sticking to the membranes inside the egg.

Power supply is therefore paramount for successful incubation. Any sustained interruption could lead to a drop in temperature and humidity, or a failure of turning, which would be fatal to the developing embryos. Back-up generators may therefore be required in areas where power-outage is a problem.

Prior to egg-laying, the hen bird will pass bulky, sloppy droppings; she may appear uncomfortable; and she will have a distended abdomen. In the

AVERAGE CLUTCH SIZES AND INCUBATION PERIODS

Species	Eggs in a clutch	Incubation (days)
African grey parrot	2–5	28–30
Blue fronted Amazon	2–5	25–28
Eclectus parrot	2–4	26–28
Senegal parrot	2–4	27–30
Pionus spp.	3–6	26–28
Pyrrhura conures	3–9	22–24
Aratinga conures	4	24
Ring-necked parakeet	3–4	22
Budgerigar	4–6	18
Cockatiel	3–7	20
Peach-faced lovebird	4–6	23
Scarlet macaw	2–4	24–28
Lesser sulphur crested cockatoo	2–3	23–27
Moluccan cockatoo	1–3	28–30

To ensure that eggs are fertile, they may be 'candled' from five to ten days after laying, to demonstrate the presence of a developing embryo. The technique involves shining a bright light through the egg in a darkened room. Initial signs of fertility would be a red circle on the yolk, followed by a progressively larger red patch in the centre of the circle, and a network of blood vessels. Eggs that are confirmed as infertile may obviously be discarded.

'Candling' an egg to see if it is fertile. A bright light is shone through to demonstrate an embryonic disc and blood vessels.

Eggs need to lose about 15 per cent of their weight as fluid over the incubation period, so regular weighing and corresponding adjustment of humidity controls are essential. Too little fluid loss and the chick can drown; too much and the egg will dry out and the embryo will dehydrate. The egg shell will harden and thereby make it difficult for the chick to break out. Failure to maintain correct humidity is probably the biggest single cause of embryonic death ('dead in shell') in artificially incubated eggs.

Hatching

For the last couple of days of the incubation period the egg turning should cease, to allow the embryo to settle in the right position for hatching. At the same time, humidity levels should be increased to 65–75 per cent to stop the membranes and embryo from drying out too quickly.

The blunt end of the egg contains a small air space, which enlarges as incubation progresses and fluid is lost. And the end of its incubation

A digital heartbeat monitor. The egg is placed in a hollow foam disc, linked to an electronic sensor. The display shows the heart rate as a number of beats per minute, and a visible graph.

period, the embryo will break through its membranous sac into this space, and start to breathe the air. This phase is known as 'internal pipping', and marks the transition from yolk-fed embryo to air-breathing chick.

The chick will start to absorb what remains of the yolk sac, prior to leaving the egg. Contraction of the abdominal muscles as the chick breathes aids this process. As the chick breathes, oxygen in the air space will become depleted, and carbon dioxide will accumulate, stimulating muscle contraction in the chick. Cheeping noises may be heard from inside the egg at this stage.

This phase may last twenty-four to forty-eight hours, but occasionally in larger birds could be as long as three or four days. Premature interference at this time on the part of the bird-keeper can lead to chick mortality, by rupturing blood vessels in the shell membrane or even damaging the yolk sac. The only attention required is observation, and the maintenance of humidity. During the latter half of incubation, the growing embryo fills more of the egg with denser material, so candling will reveal little except a dark mass. A digital heart beat monitor may be used to confirm that the embryo is still alive in the later stages of incubation, and to monitor the chick's progress during hatching.

Parrot chicks have two inbuilt aids to hatching. The first is a well-developed muscle at the back of the neck – the hatching muscle. The second is a

A newly hatched cockatoo chick, with head to the left tucked downwards, showing the fine yellow natal down, and the broad band of the 'hatching muscle' running down the back of the neck.

Newly-hatched bantam chick showing the 'egg-tooth' – a tiny projection on the upper beak that aids in breaking out of the shell. This horny outgrowth disappears within a few days of hatching.

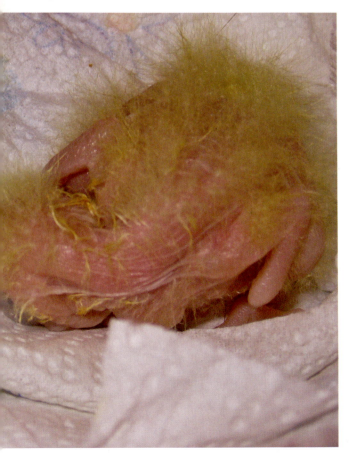

A brooder for protecting newly hatched chicks and keeping them warm.

need a constant warm environment. The newly hatched chick will rest, and resorb the remainder of its yolk sac before feeding, although it may be given a few drops of warm water with honey, or a balanced solution of oral electrolytes.

FEEDING THE CHICKS

Then the hard work begins. Once recovered from the ordeal of hatching, and dried out, the chick will need to be fed. As previously mentioned, many of the early parrot breeders prepared their own formulae, using egg biscuit, ground seeds or nuts, with cereals and fruits. It is much more efficient these days to use a proprietary prepared formula, obtained in powdered form and mixed with warm water to the right consistency.

This food should be fed comfortably warm. Adding slightly cooled boiled water to the mix usually works, and a bowl of prepared formula may be kept warm in a water bath if several birds need feeding. (The practice of heating batches of food in a microwave oven can be dangerous, resulting in 'crop burn' – *see* page 175.)

The mix may be administered via a syringe, a crop tube, or a special spoon. The blind chick will usually raise its head and beg for food as soon as there is any sound or movement. It has soft tissue on each side of the mandible ('pump pads')

Young cockatoo chick with its eyes open. The soft swellings on either side of the beak are sensitive to touch, and are known as 'pump pads'.

small protuberance on the rostrum, known as the egg tooth. As carbon dioxide levels rise, the hatching muscle starts to twitch, forcing the egg tooth against the egg shell and arching the chick's back. These combined actions will gradually split the shell and force it open – 'external pipping' – allowing the chick to escape. It is at this time that assistance may be given by removing some of the shell if necessary – but only if the chick is becoming tired, as evidenced by longer intervals between efforts or by reduced heart rate.

Eggs may be transferred at the time of pipping to the hatcher or brooder. These altricial chicks are virtually naked, blind, and unable to maintain their body temperature (thermoregulation), so will still

Parrot chick being fed with a syringe-full of formula.

A syringe with a soft plastic or rubber tube, or alternatively a ball-ended stainless steel tube may be passed directly into the crop. This method makes the feeding process a lot faster if several birds are to be fed at once, but it is unnatural to the chick. It also carries the risk of physical damage to the mouth, beak, throat or crop of these delicate birds, especially those species with a vigorous pumping reflex, like the large macaws.

The spoon method perhaps most closely approximates the natural feeding mechanism of the parent's beak. A teaspoon has its sides bent upwards

Cockatiel chick taking formula from a spoon. Note all the new feathers still in their protective sheaths, and the crop filling at the base of the neck.

which responds to touch, and the parent's beak or the feeding utensil applied here will encourage the chick to 'open wide'. If using a syringe, the plunger should be slowly pressed to squeeze out the food, which the chick will then swallow with a pumping action against the tip. The crop is easily visible in the bird's neck at this stage, and should be observed for filling. The chick will usually cease begging and relax its neck when sated, but some will over-feed if given the chance.

Stainless steel feeding tubes of different sizes. They are part curved to make passing the tube down the oesophagus easier, and the tip is ball-ended for safety.

African grey parrot chick taking food from a spoon. The vigorous 'pumping' action is conveyed by the blurring of the picture.

Cockatoo chick being spoon-fed. Note the curved sides of the feeding spoons.

Parrot chick being weighed on digital scales. Regular monitoring of bodyweight is essential to ensure an even growth rate and to detect any back-sliding.

to more readily retain its contents, and the chick is allowed to 'pump' and swallow its contents in the same way that it would receive regurgitated food from its parents' mouths.

Initially, chicks should be fed every two hours for about eighteen hours a day. It is not necessary to continue the process during six hours of darkness. The babies should be weighed regularly, at the same time and same stage (i.e. before feeding) every day, and the amount of food given should approximate to 10 per cent of the bodyweight over the course of the day. As the chicks grow and become stronger, the feeding frequency is reduced to three-hourly, then four times daily, three times daily, and eventually twice a day. The time scale of this reduction will obviously depend on the bodyweight and species of parrot. The crop will enlarge as the chick grows, so that more food of a thicker consistency may be given.

It is important that the crop be empty, or virtually so, before more food is added, otherwise there is a danger of accumulation, fermentation, and secondary infection ('sour crop'). The overnight rest should allow complete evacuation of the crop, before more food is taken. Delayed emptying is always potentially serious, and needs to be investigated.

Once the chick is down to two feeds daily, small quantities of soft food – chopped fruit and vegetables, thickened formula, soaked pulses or pellets – may be offered, and the baby parrot will gradually start to explore this new food source and begin the process of weaning. Do not force the issue: allow the chick to progress in its own time, still weighing it regularly, but gradually cutting down on the quantity of baby formula as the bird eats more by itself. The procedure is aided when several birds are raised together, or better still if older birds are present – the youngsters will learn from their older cousins.

As the chick becomes covered with down, and this is replaced in turn by proper contour feathers, the temperature of the brooder may be lowered progressively until the bird is kept at room temperature. It is also important that in the early days chicks are kept in subdued lighting except when feeding. In their natural environment, or if parent-reared in captivity, they would be lying at the bottom of a dark hole or nest box, and would see little full light until they fledge and start to climb up to the nest-hole entrance. Again, two or three decades ago it was common practice to have rooms full of parrot chicks in a production line, sitting in individual plastic tubs in a bright, white-tiled room with fluorescent lights on for most of the day.

It is important, as far as is possible, to raise baby parrots with others of their own kind. Such chicks will recognize themselves as birds and will socialize readily with others when older. Many

Cockatiel chicks being raised together, using a plastic tub as a 'nest'. Such grouping approximates the natural nesting environment, and ensures the chicks recognize and relate to other birds.

a singleton raised solely with human contact becomes a demanding imprinted parrot when older. It will not allow human owners out of its sight without screaming the place down, and fail to relate to other parrots it may encounter. The chicks' needs are far better served if they can sit together in twos and threes, in subdued lighting, with their 'nests' covered with a soft cloth in between feeds.

Plastic tubs such as those used for margarine spreads make ideal nest pans. They should be lined with soft tissue or kitchen towel, which is hygienic and easily replaced. Cotton wool is risky, as its fibres may become wrapped around the leg. Many people use wood-shavings, and whilst this substrate closely approximates that found in a natural parrot's nest, I cannot advise this material unequivocally because I have seen too many young chicks pick up and swallow pieces of wood that then get lodged in the crop. Older birds can cope with it, but until they start to develop full feathers, paper is safer.

Larger species like cockatoos or macaws may be moved on into plastic baskets as they grow. The chicks' eyes will open from ten days to three weeks old depending on species, and from this moment onwards they become much more active.

Hygiene is important: the hand-feeding of young parrots is a messy business, and feeding formula readily becomes caked on the feathers of the mouth and neck. A feeding 'bib' of kitchen

African grey chick in a plastic bin lined with wood shavings. These are hygienic and easily replaced, but are suitable only for older birds – smaller chicks may swallow wood fragments.

African grey parrot chick showing neck feathers caked with dried feeding formula. This will irritate the bird, and will become more difficult to remove the harder it sets.

RINGING

Unlike racing pigeons and birds of prey, it is not yet a legal requirement for all captive parrots to be identified by means of a closed, numbered ring (band) on their legs. However, many breeders will mark their birds in this way, so that they can trace relationships between parents and offspring.

A closed ring made of plastic, aluminium, or stainless steel will be stamped with a unique combination of letters and numbers. This usually consists of a number specific to that bird; the breeder's or society initials (e.g. PSUK – issued by The Parrot Society UK); the year of hatch; and a final code relating to ring size. Rings are issued in a range of sizes suited to different species. Plastic or aluminium rings may be coloured, and these colours are often used to relate to the year of hatch as well.

The ring must be applied after the foot has grown large enough for the ring not to slip off, but before the toes become too big to pass the ring over. For most chicks this is about seven days old. The technique is to extend the leg and the three longest toes, while holding the shortest toe back against the leg. The ring is slipped up

Racing pigeon wearing identification bands on its legs, bearing registered numbers to identify that individual bird.

over the first three toes, then further up the leg until it passes the fourth toe. The latter is then released back to its normal position, and the ring allowed to rest just above the foot. The ring must not be passed up past the hock joint: the growing leg will expand considerably at this point, and the ring will become too tight.

paper may be placed around the neck of the bird while administering the feed, and surplus should be wiped away with a clean moist tissue as soon as feeding has finished. Chicks will invariably pass droppings as soon as they have fed: this fresh waste should be removed immediately, and the lining paper or shavings changed regularly.

Plastic tubs should be disposed of or thoroughly disinfected between batches of chicks. Incubators and brooders should likewise be cleaned, disinfected, and ideally fumigated before their next use. Food mixing bowls, spoons and syringes must be washed, disinfected and stored hygienically

Mingo, Citron-crested cockatoo, with a makeshift 'bib' to avoid feeding formula caking on his neck and chest feathers.

between feeds. Human baby-bottle sterilizers containing products such as Milton® are suitable for this purpose.

POST-WEANING

Once weaned and independent, the young parrot may be settled in its new home – whether it be in your living room as a new addition to the family, or at the pet store for onward sale. If you are keeping a number of birds, the youngsters are best housed together in a 'young bird' room or aviary, where they can play together and learn avian social skills.

The practice of selling or re-homing parrots unweaned, to be 'finished-off' by the new owner, is to be discouraged. Claims that this will 'reinforce the bonding' between bird and owner are quite false. Unless the new keeper is experienced in the technique, this process is fraught with danger. Many a young parrot has succumbed to starvation, delayed weaning, damage to beak or mouth, inhalation of food leading to pneumonia, and other problems related to inexperience and poor training.

Some of the disease problems associated with the breeding and rearing of parrots are dealt with in the following chapter.

A group of young cockatoos reared and housed together, allowing them to develop avian social skills between each other.

CHAPTER 8

As Sick as a Parrot?

Whatever type of bird you keep, whether it be a single companion budgie in a cage or a large breeding collection of parrots, the objective is always to keep those birds fit and healthy. The problem is to recognize when something is going wrong, then to diagnose what that problem is, and then to be able successfully to treat the condition before it is too late. This requires vigilance and care on the part of the bird-keeper, and expertise and knowledge in the veterinarian.

Birds have a tremendous ability to mask signs of illness – they have to in nature, or they will quickly succumb to predators or attack by others of their own kind. When they do look unwell, the range of signs they show is limited: generally they will sit quietly, with feathers fluffed, eyes half closed, with loss of appetite. The challenge is to identify why

Blue and yellow macaw (Ara ararauna) *looking 'as sick as a parrot', with ruffled feathers, half-closed eyes, unkempt appearance, and squatting low on its perch.*

**CASE STUDY
HANG-UPS**

An Umbrella cockatoo lived happily in a luxury apartment with its owner, but suddenly and apparently spontaneously started to pull out his feathers. Now as we all know this is an extremely common problem in parrots, and is a complex condition that will be discussed in Chapter 10.

Before detailed examination of the bird and during careful questioning of the owner, it was revealed that he had recently moved a picture from one wall of his room to another above the bird's cage. It turned out that the bird was distressed by this change, and plucked in response. Replacing the picture to its original site resulted in an immediate cessation of plucking behaviour!

– a bird with this appearance could have any one of a dozen different conditions. Also, by the time it looks this bad, it may well be beyond saving!

Thus is it is of paramount importance for the owner to get to know the subtleties of their bird's normal behaviour – how it perches and feeds, how and when it vocalizes or preens, what its droppings look like, and how it interacts with other birds or the owner. Any change to the 'norm' is often the first sign of trouble, but such changes may be slight, and need regular observation. The story of Jack in Chapter 4 helps to illustrate this, as does the case study above.

TIME TO SEE THE VET

The next stage for the vigilant and caring owner is to enlist the services of an experienced avian veterinarian. Veterinary university education is an intensive course packed with detailed information on a whole range of species. Vets are not like human doctors, dealing just with *Homo sapiens* – we are expected to deal with anything from a hamster to an elephant and everything in between. Obviously the five or six years devoted to the training course cannot possibly encompass every detail of every disease in all species, so emphasis is given to the economically important groups – horses, cattle, pigs, sheep and goats, and dogs and cats. Smaller companion animals (rabbits, guinea pigs, hamsters) receive reasonable attention, but zoo animals, exotic pets (reptiles, insects, unusual small mammals), and birds other than commercial poultry receive only superficial attention. The situation has improved to a degree in recent years – there are more new graduates coming out with some interest in birds. And that is the key – *interest in avian medicine and bird-keeping*.

Prescription, Please

Let me introduce a few definitions. Disease or illness is any process that alters the bird's normal state of health, making it feel unwell. An infection is a disease caused by an infectious agent or germ. Contagious means that the germ can be spread from animal to animal, thus disseminating the disease. Chronic means long-standing, while acute is rapid or sudden.

Most of my clients as well as a good many veterinarians look upon any illness in a parrot as the result of an infection, and therefore request (the client) or prescribe (the vet) antibiotics. Probably only about one-third of the disease conditions we see in clinical avian practice are in fact infectious. The rest will have another cause, such as diet, environment, genetics, accident, tumours, hormones, accident or aggression, or toxins.

Of the infectious agents, some may be viruses, protozoa, or larger parasites. The rest will be bacteria, and it is only this group therefore (about 25 per cent of all cases seen) that will respond to treatment with antibiotics.

Chronic effects in the bird's body by such things as poor diet or environment may well accumulate to produce an acute crisis, which may involve secondary bacterial infection because of the bird's weakened immune system. This part of the disease may require antibiotics, but the underlying causes also have to be identified and addressed.

Sub-clinical disease is a condition that festers inside the bird without demonstrating overt clinical signs. Such long-term problems may result in poor or non-existent breeding performance; delayed, prolonged or no feather moult, or feather-plucking; kidney or liver failure; or premature death.

Symptoms are subjective feelings that can be described by the human patient. Thus a human can communicate 'a stabbing pain', a 'buzzing in the ears', a 'feeling of nausea', a pain like a 'tight band around the head'. Birds cannot describe what they feel: they can only show objective signs, such as lameness, vomiting or scratching, to be observed by the owner or veterinarian.

Because birds have the aforementioned ability to mask signs of disease until it is almost too late, further valuable time can be lost by the 'try this antibiotic and see if it works' approach. Precise diagnosis from the word go is much more valuable, and this is where the veterinarian's expertise comes in. All veterinary students are taught the value of 'history taking' – the process of questioning the owner about the animal and its presenting problem. We have to play detective and gather many clues from various sources, part of which would be background history and owner information. Look at the previously-quoted example of the plucking cockatoo – the diagnosis was made pretty much by the questioning of the owner as to what had changed, and was proven by the bird's response to the picture's replacement.

Case History

The background history will include such information as the species, age and sex of the bird. How long has it been owned and where did it come from? How is it housed and what food is it given?

Young Blue and yellow macaw showing the rounded head and smaller beak of the juvenile bird.

Adults have a longer, flatter head and a much larger rostrum in proportion to the mandible.

We have learned from previous chapters how all of these factors can influence the type of disease occurring.

Recently imported birds, or those acquired from pet shops, dealers, or at a bird show, may show illness resulting from stress and contagious infections; while those acquired quietly from a private source or bred yourself should be reasonably healthy. If from a pet-store, have any diagnostic tests already been carried out, such as psittacosis, DNA sexing, or PBFD (psittacine beak and feather disease)? A recently acquired bird may have problems with settling in, resulting in stress-related conditions, while a bird that you have had for thirty years could be suffering from chronic deficiency disease or environmental factors such as smoke.

How old is the bird? Just as human babies and children will show a different range of problems to the doctor than do adults and pensioners, so young birds will suffer from conditions that are unlikely to afflict an old bird, and vice versa. Good examples are PBFD virus in young African grey parrots, or arthritis in old parrots. In many cases the age of the bird is known because of a provided hatch date, or a year suffix on a leg ring, but very often this knowledge is not available, and then we have to estimate how old the patient is. Differences in

plumage, eye colour, or beak shape associated with age have been discussed in earlier chapters.

The sex of the parrot is obviously important (see below for diseases associated with sex and breeding).

Diet and Droppings

Next we would need to discuss the bird's diet. So many of the problems we see are related to diet in some way – unbalanced, deficient in important items, too high in fat, too much, too little, poor quality, containing toxic items, or just completely wrong for the bird. Nutritional requirements and the feeding of parrots were covered in Chapter 6. The food can be responsible for making a bird actively sick; or weakening its immune system so that it is vulnerable to infection; or resulting in chronic disease from the lack of various essential nutrients.

The basic quality of the food is important: seed-based mixes come in varying prices, according to their constituents, and the efficiency of the cleaning process, and this was also discussed in Chapter 6. Once it is purchased, storage is important. Contamination with dust, mould, or rodent urine and droppings will all potentially cause ill health in

DESTROYING THE EVIDENCE

The last thing we do always when we go to the dentist is to clean our teeth. Similarly, owners like to clean their bird's cage before they take it to the vet, so that we do not think they are neglecting their pet or keeping it in squalid conditions. I ask my clients not to do this, because it can get rid of important diagnostic clues.

I will question the owner about the food that is fed, and they may list a whole range of 'good' items presented to the bird, but when one looks at the cage it is clear that the bird is dumping most of these items on the floor and just selecting the stuff he likes. Similarly, we can see how much or how little the bird may be eating out of what is presented, and also look for signs of vomiting, bleeding or discharges.

your birds. The same applies to quality of drinking water. Fresh water should be available at all times, and we all know that birds will dunk food, droppings, and bedding material in their water, producing a thick soup of disease-forming organisms, especially in hot weather.

Mice and rats will contaminate parrots' food with their urine and droppings, spreading potentially serious infectious diseases.

Having discussed what goes in at the front end of the bird, we now turn our attention to what comes out at the back. Birds and reptiles pass a combined 'dropping' which is a mixture of waste products from the kidneys and the bowel. The kidney waste is primarily urate, a semi-solid white substance, together with some true liquid urine. The material passed from the gut after digestion is mixed with this as a coil of brown, green, or black material. The relative proportions of these components will vary with species, diet, time of day and breeding cycle. Small seed eaters pass a small, dry, black and white dropping; nectar feeders pass very fluid droppings. The first dropping of the day is

Normal droppings from a budgerigar – a small, dry pellet of dark faecal material mixed with white/yellow urate. There is hardly any liquid component.

Normal parrot dropping from a bird on a seed-based diet. The faecal component is dark green/black, mixed with bright white urate, and surrounded by a liquid urine.

Similar colours and proportions, but more of them. This would be the first dropping of the day as the parrot wakes, or that laid by a hen in egg-laying mode. In both examples, the cloaca stretches to accommodate a greater volume.

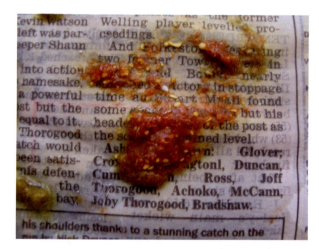

Droppings containing red colour (and undigested seeds) following the ingestion of peppers.

However, we do look closely for signs of soft, pale faecal material – indicating a bowel dysfunction, possibly enteritis. Very bulky, pasty faeces can be a sign of pancreatic or liver disease. Urates that should be white but instead are yellow or green indicate liver or kidney damage; an increase in liquid urine in a previously drier dropping may be a sign of diabetes or kidney disease. Undigested food items coming straight through would suggest serious bowel dysfunction, while blood may indicate acute infection, foreign body, ulcer or tumour,

This dropping shows normal bright white urate, with some urine, but pale green sloppy faecal material. This bird has diarrhoea.

By contrast, this sample shows normal dark green coils of faecal waste, but the urate fraction is copious and stained green. This bird will have kidney or liver disease.

usually bulky and sloppy, as is that passed by an egg-laying hen. Food pigments may colour either the urate or the faecal part – blackberries, beetroot, and chillies for example. A bird that is stressed will pass a very liquid dropping.

So there is considerable variation in appearance of droppings that could still be considered as normal. Once again, we need to know what is normal before we can diagnose the abnormal – another situation where the cage or carry box can provide clues!

This sample has profuse liquid urate/urine which is very discoloured, indicating serious liver dysfunction.

A parrot dropping with a very small faecal component, a very little white urate, and a large volume of liquid urine. This may come from a nectar-eating bird like a lory, but in this particular case the bird was diabetic.

egg-related problems, or heavy metal poisoning. Passage of roundworms or tapeworms needs no explanation. All these are grossly visible at the time of examination, but can give us vital clues as to which direction to proceed diagnostically. The droppings may be examined in more detail in the laboratory, but at least we have some early signs.

OK, so we have come a long way by asking all these questions about the bird and its diet and husbandry, and during this time the experienced veterinarian should also be watching the bird. These several minutes will have given it time to relax, and it may then show signs that were hidden when it first came in because it was stressed and excited. Owners always want to plonk their birds on the table and immediately get them out to show the vet, but I insist on this preliminary period to allow the bird to calm down. Then we can see it beginning to fluff its feathers and close its eyes; scratch itself or over-preen repeatedly; breathe heavily with tail bobbing; attempt to vomit; hold its leg up; or even fall off the perch.

This is also a good reason to justify the added time and expense of a house-call to see the bird in its own home environment: we can pick up much more information then as to how the bird is being kept. This is especially useful when dealing with behavioural problems.

Handling the Patient

At this stage of the proceedings, the experienced veterinarian should have a good idea of what is going on with the bird, and will then decide what further diagnostic tests and possible treatments may be required. It is now that the patient will be handled. The catching and handling of the bird is an important skill that can make or break a vet's reputation with birds. Quiet confidence and ability will reduce the stress for all concerned

The handling period should be kept to a minimum, especially if respiratory distress has already been noted. Everything that may be needed – sampling instruments, injections – should be ready to hand. The bird certainly should not be held for many minutes, while waving the hand and bird up and down to emphasize a point to the owner, especially if the bird is suffering from breathing problems. This actually happened on one TV vet programme, and of course the unfortunate cockatiel died.

There is no doubt that modern techniques such as diagnostic imaging all have their place in precise diagnosis, but they should not be used on every case just because they are available in the practice. Common sense and basic handling, coupled with a

Freddie, Green-cheeked conure held securely and comfortably in the hand for examination.

A more recent photograph of the author, with another Umbrella cockatoo, restrained in a towel.

The author (picture taken several years ago!) with an Umbrella cockatoo, relaxed and comfortable with being held by a stranger.

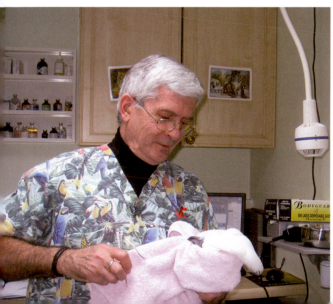

thorough history should give a diagnosis in at least 50 per cent of cases.

This is a long explanation of diagnosis that can take place in fifteen or twenty minutes in the clinic! I hope I have managed to convey something of the wealth of information that is required from the owner and has to be investigated by the vet in order to make a diagnosis of the numerous possible disease conditions that can afflict our birds.

It is only by early detection and correct diagnosis that we can provide the right treatment and hopefully cure the bird. However, as I always say, we are dealing with biological grey all the time – there is no cut and dried black or white. The same condition can affect two different birds, and one may live while the other dies. Multiple problems can occur in one individual, all adding to the joy and frustration of bird-keeping and veterinary practice.

COMMON DISEASES

It should by now be obvious that a large proportion of disease problems in parrots result from dietary and environmental influences. Infectious conditions are important, and will also be covered, together with important steps to take in the prevention, control and elimination of disease from your birds. This is not a veterinary textbook, and will not therefore catalogue every disease encountered. I shall describe some of those most likely to be met by the average parrot-keeper.

Dietary Diseases

The nutritional requirements and feeding techniques for captive parrots were covered in Chapter 6. Most disease problems are the result of long-term dietary imbalance. Minor irregularities may show as long-term poor growth and development, poor quality plumage or breeding performance. More marked changes will manifest as specific disease entities.

Food Deficiencies

By far the most common important food items lacking in parrots' diets are vitamin A and

Young Ring-necked parakeet (Psittacula krameri) *showing an enlarged nostril following the removal of a keratinous plug that was the result of long-term deficiency of vitamin A.*

Calcium. Both these substances are found in low quantity in the standard seed-based 'parrot-mix', so birds that select this diet – or are given nothing else – will inevitably develop problems in time. Hypovitaminosis-A will have damaging effects on the lining membranes of mouth, nose and throat, as well as the kidneys. Gradually these membranes become thickened and secondarily infected,

Very poor feather condition in an Amazon parrot with chronic deficiency disease. Feathers are unsheathed and do not lie smoothly together. The sole of the foot is smooth and thin-skinned instead of having a rough surface.

Swelling in the face of an African grey parrot, associated with discharges from the eye and nostril.

The swelling incised to reveal a caseous (cheesy) plug, or sinus abscess, again the result of chronic vitamin A deficiency. The subsequent secondary infection leads to the nasal and ocular discharges.

showing as enlarged, blocked nostrils, 'abscesses' in the tongue or facial sinuses, or kidney failure. The caseous (cheesy) accumulations will need to be removed, and the parrot's diet improved and supplemented with vitamin A.

Hypocalcaemia can have many profound effects depending on its severity and the stage of life at which it develops. Breeding parrots may have no eggs, or soft-shelled eggs; hens that do produce

A severe example of metabolic bone disease in a young African grey parrot. The leg and wing bones are soft and bent, meaning that the bird cannot stand and support its own weight.

eggs may become egg-bound as their muscles weaken easily; growing chicks may have soft, deformed bones ('rickets'). Adult birds will have muscle tremors or weakness, finding it difficult to hang on to their perches. More severely affected birds will have epileptiform attacks or 'fits', lasting two or three minutes. The bird will fall suddenly to the floor, squawking and flapping frantically. Gradually it will relax and calm down, remaining limp and motionless, before slowly regaining consciousness, finding its feet, and climbing back up the cage. The patient may break claws or feathers in the process, and will often bruise the facial skin or eye ridges.

African Grey and Eclectus parrots are most frequently affected: they seem either to have a greater need for calcium than other species, or are less efficient at metabolizing it. Of the panic 'phone calls I get from anxious owners or veterinarians describing an African grey as 'falling from its perch' or 'having a fit', 95 per cent turn out to be caused by calcium deficiency problems, and respond rapidly to therapy with calcium.

Eating to Excess

Many captive parrots eat far too much food, resulting in an excessive intake of carbohydrates and fats. If human junk food is a part of this intake, the problem will be made much worse. Affected birds will appear rotund, with yellow fat deposits showing through their thin skin. This is just the tip of the iceberg – similar accumulations will occur inside the body around the internal organs, resulting in pressure and malfunction, as well as difficulty in breathing because of reduced capacity of the air sacs. The liver and kidneys particularly will become infiltrated with fat cells, seriously compromising their function. This is in turn often reflected in overgrowth and flaking of the beak, or haemorrhage within its substance. Major blood vessels will become thickened with fat in their walls, just as they do in humans, leading to increase in blood pressure, reduced exercise ability, breathlessness, and heart failure. Increased bodyweight will put extra strain on joints and ligaments.

The prime culprits are Amazon parrots, Roseate cockatoos, and budgerigars. These are all species

*Sub-cutaneous yellow fat deposits clearly visible through the skin of this Amboina king parakeet (*Alisterus amboinensis*), submitted for autopsy.*

Adult male budgerigar (blue cere) with spots of chronic haemorrhage within the layers of its beak, showing as dark splodges. These are associated with advanced liver disease: this bird had a liver tumour.

that will eat all day if allowed, and often select the high-fat food items. Prolonged fat-deposition – especially in budgerigars – will often lead to the formation of fatty tumours, or lipomata.

Toxins

Poisons may be ingested (eaten) or inhaled. Swallowed agents include avocado (see Chapter 7), causing gastro-enteritis and nervous signs; and heavy metals such as zinc and lead (see Chapter 4) causing haemorrhagic enteritis and nervous signs. The inquisitive nature of most parrots means that they will often nibble at things that should not concern them, and make themselves ill as a result. Continual vigilance is required on the part of the owner to ensure that household items like electric cables, small metal objects, or other potentially dangerous items are kept out of the bird's reach. Toxic houseplants or outdoor vegetation accessible to aviary birds may also be a problem.

We learned in Chapter 1 how sensitive the parrot's respiratory system is to inhaled gases. Carbon monoxide, coal gas, cigarette or bonfire smoke, aerosol sprays, and paint fumes will all cause problems to birds. There may be transient coughing or choking, 'asthmatic' attacks, or chronic respiratory disease with prolonged exposure. Perhaps the most toxic and dramatic are the fumes given off by overheated non-stick pan linings (like Teflon®) or cooking oil. As described in Chapter 5, such occurrences will kill a parrot within minutes.

Tumours

Many types of tumour are found in parrots, but budgerigars are perhaps the most susceptible.

The ubiquitous Dougal destroying a TV remote control. Such household items are a potential hazard to parrots, apart from the nuisance of having your home destroyed!

Assorted tumours in parrots: 1 Cancer of the preen gland in a budgerigar. 2 and 3 Xanthomata (tumours of cholesterol-based fatty tissue) in cockatiels. 4 Skin cancer in an Amazon parrot. 5 Nasal tumour in a white-fronted Amazon parrot.

These may be internal, and would include growths in the liver, ovary or testes, or occasionally other organs. Tumours affecting the gonads will often manifest as lameness, as well as a swollen abdomen.

Alternatively they may be external, affecting the skin, feathers, or preen gland. Most skin tumours are benign accumulations of fat (lipomata), or cholesterol (xanthomata), but others may be aggressive skin cancers or localized nodular fibrous tumours. Others may be virus-linked (papillomata – *see* below).

Virus Diseases

There are several of these minute, infectious, intracellular organisms that will cause specific diseases

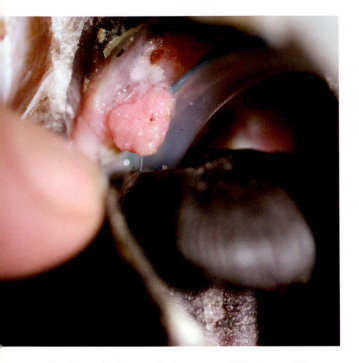

Papilloma in the mouth of a macaw. This is a cauliflower-like warty growth, next to the blue/grey plastic endotracheal tube inserted into the bird's windpipe. The large, dark grey, fleshy tongue typical of most parrots is in the foreground.

A common herpes virus causes an acute, rapidly fatal, hepatitis in parrots, and is known as Pacheco's disease. This is most frequently encountered in recently imported birds in quarantine. It will spread rapidly and will wipe out a high percentage of the group in a few days.

Polyomavirus generally afflicts young parrots, and will result in sudden death, with pale skin and pin-point haemorrhages visible in the skin and around abdominal organs. Any birds that do survive (especially budgerigars) generally develop abnormal stunted feathering.

Circovirus is the cause of the highly unpleasant psittacine beak and feather disease (PBFD). This virus attacks young growing feather and beak tissue in fledgling birds, as well as damaging their immune system, so they have no resistance to other diseases. In budgerigars it is known as French moult, and although most infected birds will die, some will survive but with damaged wing and tail feathers, so they can never fly and are hence known as runners. In most other parrots, infection is almost invariably fatal. The course of the disease varies with the age at infection and the infective dose of virus. Very young chicks will die quickly, often dropping feathers by the

Citron-crested cockatoo Ari showing typical stunted, clubbed feathers of PBFD infection, with loss of normal contour. The pale brown iris is typical of the hen in white cockatoos, and the ear opening is exposed owing to the loss of feather cover.

in parrots. Some that are found in other birds, like avian influenza, are infrequently encountered in parrots.

Pox virus is occasionally seen in macaws, producing crusty lesions on the facial skin. Adenoviruses generally result in liver disease (hepatitis), and particularly affect lovebirds. Paramyxovirus will affect the nervous systems of small grass parakeets (*Neophema* species), manifesting as head tilt and circling, with loss of balance. This virus occurs commonly in pigeons and doves, and these birds therefore may be a source of infection to parakeets. A vaccine produced to protect pigeons has been used with some success in vulnerable and valuable flocks of parakeets.

In poultry, many tumours are virus-induced, and it is quite likely that similar viruses of the leucosis group are responsible for tumours in budgerigars and cockatiels. Papillomavirus certainly produces wart-like growths in the cloaca and oral cavity.

African grey parrot with PBFD, showing loss of normal wing and tail feathers, and pink discolouration of the normally grey feathers.

Chronic PBFD-affected cockatoo with no normal feathers and overgrown, deformed beak.

handful first. Older birds will develop characteristic feather deformities or discolourations – white in black birds like the Vasa parrot or pink in African greys.

Young Umbrella cockatoo showing grubby feathering, depression, and shiny beak – the early stages of PBFD.

In older birds, the disease can be more protracted. In the early stages, birds may show depression, vague dirty discolouration of the feathers, and a loss of powder down. This will show as a black shiny beak instead of the normal dusty

Advanced PBFD cockatoo with virtually no feathers. The body of these birds is remarkably small when the plumage is removed.

grey. More advanced cases show further feather and beak deformity, and ultimately loss of most of the plumage. There is currently no cure, and all infected parrots will die of this disease (if they are not put to sleep on welfare grounds before) of organ failure or secondary infections. The longest I have known a clinically infected bird to survive is fifteen years.

The virus occurs naturally in wild parrots in Australasia, but spread rapidly through captive populations in the 1980s and early 1990s, when large groups of young parrots were hand-reared together. The disease can show itself after an incubation period of ten days, but it can also remain dormant for many months, so infected birds were sold on before it was realized that they were infected.

The clinical signs of the abnormal feathers are distinctive: other clues are a profound drop in white cell blood count; histological examination of feather pulp; or a PCR test (polymerase chain reaction) to detect virus DNA. The virus is spread in infected feather dust, so care should be taken when handling suspect birds.

Avian bornavirus is responsible for another devastating disease with a prolonged incubation period – macaw wasting disease (so-called because it was first identified commonly in macaws), or proventricular dilatation disease (PDD) or proventricular dilatation syndrome (PDS). This virus

Whole seed kernels passed in parrot droppings, indicative of digestive dysfunction, often proventricular dilatation disease (PDD).

is similar in its effects to Key-Gaskell syndrome in cats or grass sickness in horses. Initial infection causes mild transient diarrhoea, from which most individuals recover. In a small percentage, there is damage to the nerves controlling the stomach, so that this organ becomes stretched, thin-walled and bloated. Digestive efficiency is impaired, so affected birds will eat well but lose weight, commonly vomit, and will pass undigested food items (especially seed kernels) in their droppings. Some birds will also show nervous signs such as tremors or incoordination. Like PBFD, the incubation period can be many months, making the source of infection difficult to define. It is also currently incurable, although isolated pet birds may be maintained by feeding soft foods and giving non-steroidal anti-inflammatory drugs (NSAIDs).

All these viral diseases have no specific treatments, since antibiotics will have no effect. Thus their control depends on vaccination (where possible, and currently such availability is very limited); hygiene and disinfection; and quarantine. It is important not to mix newly-acquired birds with existing stock until they have been kept in isolation for a period of quarantine to allow dormant infections to show themselves. This period should be from ten to thirty days, the longer the better. Most infectious agents will show up in this time, but as mentioned with PBFD and PDD, some viruses

White feather dust on a veterinarian's scrub top after handling a cockatoo. This would be a risk to other birds if it came from a bird infected with PBFD virus.

will incubate for many months. However, parrots can be tested during the quarantine period for the presence of these viruses. Such control measures apply equally to other infectious diseases.

Psittacosis

Psittacosis is a common and potentially serious disease occurring in both the birds that we keep and the humans that keep them, but there is still a lot that is misunderstood about the condition. The causal organism has recently been re-named *Chlamydophila psittaci* (originally *Chlamydia psittaci)*, and is found in a wide variety of birds and mammals, including man. This species is now sub-divided into many sub-species, each affecting a different animal. The blanket term for the disease produced by *Chlamydophila psittaci* affecting all species is chlamydiosis; if it occurs in a bird it is properly known as ornithosis; and when found specifically in psittacine birds it is termed psittacosis. This latter is the name with which we are more familiar, and it has by popular usage been stretched to cover the disease occurring in all animals, including man.

The organism itself is unusual in that it has certain characteristics of bacteria – that is, it is relatively large and is sensitive to antibiotics; but it also resembles viruses in that it can grow and multiply only within the cells of its host. Damage is then caused by the rupture of these cells and the release of toxins into the system. *Chlamydophila* appear to infect and multiply in most types of cell, hence the widely variable disease pattern seen in different individuals or species.

The organism will survive outside the host for approximately one month if protected by cell debris and protein material (droppings, nasal discharges). An important aspect of disease control therefore is cleanliness and disinfection to remove such debris. Efficient disinfectants are the quaternary ammonium compounds; benzalkonium chloride; and those that are formalin based. Thus the conventional fumigation of quarantine premises with formaldehyde gas (formalin and potassium permanganate) is very effective against this organism, provided surfaces have first been adequately cleaned.

Natural occurrence of infection is world-wide, and it is estimated that *1 per cent* of wild birds are infected and act as carriers. Many birds can hold the organism in their bodies in a latent state without showing signs of the disease – these birds are carriers, and are a persistent risk to other birds. Carriers appear to be especially common in collections of budgerigars, where infection rates have been reported to be as high as *30 per cent*. In the wild state, with birds living in equilibrium with their environment, the disease appears to cause little problem.

It is only when outside pressures result in stress that illness strikes. Thus loss of food sources or habitat will precipitate disease, as will capture, transport, quarantine and re-housing. The disease is therefore most commonly encountered after recent importation or moving of premises. At this time, birds are stressed and weakened, and the individuals carrying *Chlamydophila* start to shed the organisms in their droppings. Birds in these situations are often in closer confinement and proximity than in nature, and contagion occurs rapidly. The spread of infection is largely airborne in feather and faecal dust which is then inhaled by susceptible animals. A bird which looks perfectly bright and healthy to both seller and purchaser at the time of sale, but which is nonetheless infected as a carrier, could therefore become unwell with this disease after it moves to the new premises. Worse, it could infect already established birds in the new home with which it comes in contact.

The incubation period (this is the time from infection with the organism to the onset of visible clinical signs) however, is extremely variable, and this can cause considerable confusion and distress when attempting to pinpoint a source of infection. The minimum interval is possibly only ten days. At the same time an infected bird will start shedding *Chlamydophila* (thus passing on the infection) ten days before it shows signs of illness itself, thus being a risk to adjacent birds while it still appears 'healthy'. The maximum incubation period is almost open ended – times from nine months to one and a half years have been recorded.

It therefore follows that a bird could be in contact with *Chlamydophila* at any time during breeding, transfer to the wholesaler, pet shop or new owner, and that clinical signs may develop at any one of these stages. It is then very difficult to confirm the source of infection. You may also have a carrier bird sitting in your collection for years until some stress such as a change of diet, or rebuilding of flights triggers the shedding of the organism. In this way an outbreak can occur in an apparently 'closed' flock, even if no new birds have been brought into the collection.

Clinical signs are many and variable, depending on species involved, and the intensity of the infection. Cockatiels and Neophema parakeets will often exhibit a persistent conjunctivitis and blepharitis (sore eyes with swollen eyelids) but with few other clinical signs. Very susceptible birds may be found suddenly dead, but the classic clinical picture is the 'sick parrot', with depression, ruffled feathers, loss of weight, inappetance, diarrhoea and respiratory symptoms. The latter usually include thick nasal discharge with a sneeze; and the diarrhoea is typically bright fluorescent green. It seems that the initial condition of the bird when infected and the size of the infective dose are more important to the progress of the disease than is the species of bird involved.

The difficulty in making a clinical diagnosis, however, is that not all of these signs may be present, and conversely there are many other systemic infections that can produce a similar picture. Accurate diagnosis must be supported by further laboratory tests, and herein lies more difficulty. Most tests take time to achieve a result, often too late for the bird; or the tests themselves are not conclusive. It is often necessary to take blood and dropping samples, and submit them to a range of tests. A single negative result does not conclusively mean the bird does not have the disease, since the organism is shed only intermittently from its intracellular home. The result simply means that *Chlamydophila* were not present in that particular sample on the day of testing.

Once the problem of making a positive diagnosis is overcome, we then have to make a decision over treatment: whether or not to treat at all, depending on the circumstances; and then we have to choose the right medication for a long enough period. There is a strong case to argue that a bird affected with psittacosis should be put to sleep, since the disease is highly contagious, difficult to eliminate, and a threat to human health. Thus in the quarantine or pet shop situation, where many other birds are involved, and infestation can be difficult to eliminate from a premises, it is perhaps wiser to cull infected birds. This should be followed by a regime of disinfection and testing for carrier birds (subject to the limitations described above).

Cockatiel showing conjunctivitis and blepharitis (swollen inflamed eyelid), a common sign of psittacosis in this species.

Droppings from a parrot with psittacosis. The faecal component is sloppy and sparse, indicating reduced appetite, while the urate fraction is stained bright fluorescent green with bile pigments.

On the other hand, when the patient is a much-loved pet, and especially where signs are not severe, treatment can be attempted. One must take into account the human risk factor: if there are young people in the household, or people with breathing difficulties such as asthma or bronchitis, then it should be considered wiser to put the bird to sleep rather than risk their lives.

Although antibodies to the organism can be detected in the blood of both birds and man, these merely indicate exposure to infection, and they apparently have little protective effect. Thus there is no lasting immunity produced, and individuals (avian and human) can be re-infected almost as soon as they have recovered, if exposed to the organism again. For similar reasons, there is at present no way of vaccinating to prevent the disease, because of the lack of any ability to stimulate immunity.

If treatment is attempted, the drug of choice on the whole is one of the tetracycline group, to which the chlamydial organism is sensitive. *However, the drug has to be administered in a form that produces an effective dose for a sufficient treatment period.* The antibiotic will act only on the organisms when they are growing and multiplying, and since the *Chlamydophila* can exist dormant in cells for some time, the drug will be useless at these periods. It is therefore recommended that medication be sustained for a minimum of thirty-five to forty-five days to be effective in eliminating the infection. Treatment for shorter periods of five to ten days will often produce a rapid clinical improvement, but the bird is *not cured*, and can either relapse into disease, or remain a carrier to transmit infection to other stock.

This prolonged use of antibiotic can itself pose problems of imbalance of the normal intestinal flora, producing diarrhoea and malabsorption conditions, or secondary infection by opportunist fungi or yeasts. There may be also some immuno-suppressive effects from the drug; and it can be difficult to maintain therapeutically effective levels of the tetracycline within the cells. Tetracycline reacts with calcium in the diet to limit its absorption, so birds have to be given low levels of calcium during the treatment period, otherwise the antibiotic is useless.

The choice of tetracycline type and its route of administration is the next problem posed. Obviously if a flock of birds is involved, it is much easier to medicate in bulk orally, through feed or drinking water. The difficulty here is that water-soluble forms of tetracycline are fairly unstable, and will lose their potency very quickly unless solutions are changed regularly. There is also the problem of ensuring that the birds take in enough to be therapeutically effective.

In the USA there are available seeds and pellets impregnated with tetracyclines. These can be more effective than water medication, provided the birds take the diet. Fussy eating or even starvation can result when birds will not co-operate.

Injectable treatments are more therapeutically efficient, but also have their problems. The technique involves handling and therefore stressing the birds at regular intervals, and this may be impractical when large numbers or small birds are concerned. Some degree of muscle damage is often experienced with these injections: the damage is usually reversible, but it is nevertheless an unpleasant side-effect.

There has also been some success in the treatment of psittacosis using the newer quinolone antibiotics such as enrofloxacin (Baytril) and its derivatives. This drug is more palatable and stable in the drinking water, and the injectable form is less likely to produce muscle damage than the tetracyclines. However, there is also evidence to suggest that apparent 'cures' are in fact just clinical improvements with the birds still remaining infected and acting as carriers.

Thus psittacosis is a disease that has long been recognized, and yet is still not fully understood. The clinical picture is variable; the incubation period can be exceptionally long; carrier birds complicate the epidemiology; and precise diagnosis can be difficult. Treatment is available and can be effective if instituted correctly, but the decision on whether to treat must be carefully made, depending on the number of birds involved, the environment, and the risk to humans. Any person associated with birds who develops 'flu-like signs should always alert their doctor to the avian connection, and therefore the possibility of psittacosis, in order to allow an early diagnosis to be made.

Bacterial Diseases

Because of the 'open' nature of a parrot's anatomy, with no muscular diaphragm to separate the chest cavity from the abdomen, and free communication between the air sac system and the hollow bones (*see* Chapter 1), most introduced infectious organisms may start in one organ like the lung or the stomach, but will rapidly spread around the body to produce a septicaemia.

The list of possible bacteria is long, and precise identification would depend upon laboratory culture and analysis. Such tests can include antibiotic sensitivity, revealing which antibacterial drug should theoretically kill the organism. The choice will be tempered by cost, availability, possible side-effects, and the practicalities of its administration to the patient. Drugs given in drinking water are often not taken in sufficient dose by the bird; palatable in-food medications are few and far between; while the daily administration of drops, tablets, or injections is stressful for the parrot and the owner.

Common bacteria include the enteric 'food-poisoning' organisms *Salmonella* and *E. coli; Klebsiella, Yersinia, Mycobacteria* (tuberculosis) and many others. Because of the range of organs involved, infected birds will generally show the generic 'sick parrot' appearance, being fluffed up, subdued, inappetant, and with loose, discoloured droppings.

Fungal Diseases

Yeast organisms like *Candida albicans* cause disease of the digestive system, often following antibiotic usage or damage to the immune system. Hand-reared chicks are commonly affected, with thrush appearing as yellow plaques in the mouth; or infections of the crop, with thickenings of the lining with creamy yellow-deposits. Older parrots may have smelly, pasty diarrhoea, and stained impression smears of their droppings will show large quantities of yeast organisms.

Aspergillosis is caused by the inhalation of fungal spores that grow inside the bird as a fungal plaque in the lungs or on the air sacs. Such spores are present continually in the air we breathe: small numbers of spores are eliminated by protective white blood cells in the body. Active infection arises either if large quantities are inhaled, such as when mould grows on food or droppings left in the cage or aviary, or the parrot cracks open a stale nut; or if the bird's immune system is weakened by poor diet or virus infection. It is very common to find Aspergillosis in young African grey parrots: many of these birds turn out to be infected with PBFD virus.

The fungus causes disease in two ways. Firstly the physical presence of the mould growth will affect the bird's breathing. Fungal colonies developing at the base of the trachea (windpipe) result

Mould growing on peaches. Each black dot is a capsule containing thousands of tiny infective fungal spores.

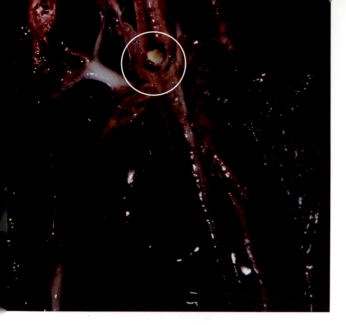

Post-mortem dissection of the neck of a parrot showing a yellow fungal granuloma growing at the base of the trachea, choking the bird.

Budgerigar with chronic vomiting problems. The sticky material cakes the feathers around the head and neck. Such a problem is commonly the result of infection with either trichomonas or megabacteria.

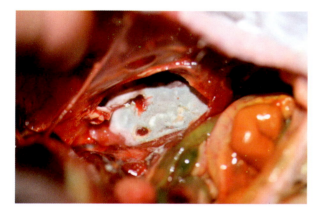

Grey-green fungal growth in the thoracic air sac of a parrot.

in an acute, choking problem, with rapid death if there is no emergency treatment. Growth in the lungs will lead to pneumonia, while that in the air-sacs will cause more insidious, gradual breathing problems. Meanwhile, the fungal colony releases a toxin into the blood stream that attacks the liver, causing death by toxic hepatitis.

Megabacterium (Macrorhabdus ornithogaster) is an organism something between a bacterium and a fungus, which is treated with a combination of antibiotics and anti-fungal drugs. Its most common manifestation is as a chronic digestive disease in budgerigars, with vomiting and weight loss.

Parasites

These may be external or internal, and are generally larger organisms living on body tissues of their host.

Internal parasites include protozoa and coccidia, although these tend to be less of a problem in parrots than in poultry and other bird species. The exception is *Trichomonas,* which causes canker in pigeons or frounce in birds of prey. This organism will also frequently infect budgerigars, resulting in chronic vomiting and weight loss, similar to megabacteriosis.

Tapeworms are seen occasionally in recently imported African grey parrots or cockatoos, and will appear protruding from the vent as a creamy-grey wriggly ribbon just 2–3mm across.

Roundworms are far more common, especially in ground-feeding birds like grass parakeets and some cockatoos. They may be passed in the droppings, and are visible, appearing as 2–3cm long, pointed at both ends.

External parasites include ticks, lice and mites. *Ticks* live for much of the year resting in vegetation, but will climb to find a suitable host when

Roundworms in droppings from a Galah cockatoo.

Mites from the skin of a bird. Like ticks, they have eight legs, and are very active.

they require a meal of blood. They are found particularly in areas where there are sheep, rabbits, or hedgehogs, and most vulnerable are parrots in outside aviaries with overhanging plants. The ticks will attach to the unwary bird by way of their sharp, barbed mouthparts and suck blood over the next few days, swelling in size as they do. Once sated, they will drop off, but they inject an anticoagulant into the puncture site. Some birds will react to this substance, and will be found suddenly dead with no previous signs of illness. The tick may or may not still be attached. Control of this problem depends on the removal of overgrown vegetation from around the flight.

Lice and mites living on the feathers and skin are far less common in parrots than they are in species like canaries, poultry and pigeons. However, quill mites that live within the feather may be a cause

'Scaly face' in a budgerigar. This an infestation with the burrowing mite Cnemidocoptes pilae, *resulting in crusty proliferations in infected areas.*

Tick removed from a bird. It is lying on its back, revealing its eight legs and central mouth parts.

A more severe case, with secondary overgrowth of the beak. The 'tunnels' in the keratin used by the mites may be clearly seen.

thickened skin in affected areas. Historic treatments include the use of liquid paraffin or petroleum jelly, which will have the effect of suffocating the mites; or benzyl benzoate applications, which gradually will kill the parasite. However, these treatments require prolonged, repeated applications to achieve success. Current medication is by application of the parasiticide *ivermectin*. This is absorbed through the bird's skin, and kills the mite via the bloodstream. Generally two applications ten to fourteen days apart will be successful, although in severe cases a third may be required. The infestation appears not to be highly contagious: only a few individuals in a flock may show signs. There appears to be a need for immuno-suppression in the bird before the mite can multiply sufficiently to show clinical disease.

of some feather-plucking problems. The most common external parasite found in parrots is the scaly face/leg mite *Cnemidocoptes*, and this is most frequently encountered in budgerigars. This is similar to the mange mites of cats, dogs and foxes, and burrows into the skin, resulting in crusty

FIRST AID CARE

It should by now be obvious that there are many disease conditions that can potentially affect your birds. Precise diagnosis and specific treatment is the province of an experienced avian veterinarian, but several commonsense precautions may be taken to avoid such problems. These include

This same yellow bird also had infestation by the mite of its feet and lower legs – 'scaly leg'. Again there is proliferative keratinized tissue present.

Infra-red lamp used to supply heat to a sick bird – in this case an African grey parrot. The lamp is mounted to one end of the cage, allowing the bird to move away if it becomes too hot.

CASE STUDY: A CAUTIONARY TALE

One of my clients some years ago had imported a batch of African grey parrots to set up a breeding collection. A number of the birds were infected with *Salmonella* bacteria, and one in particular became quite ill.

The client did well to spot the problem, obtain a proper diagnosis, and institute appropriate treatment to the birds. This all reinforces my comments earlier about observation of your birds and making the correct diagnosis, and isolating the patient. The very sick individual was placed in a cage with an infra-red lamp suspended above him, and in due course he made a full recovery from the bacterial infection. There is no doubt that the heat-lamp played a part in this treatment.

However, the lamp was suspended just above the cage and its single perch. The parrot had nowhere to go to escape the infra-red rays. As a result it sustained a scorching injury to its scalp. The second lesson therefore, is that the use of a heat lamp is invaluable, but it should be positioned such that the bird can move away from it as it recovers. If suspended above the cage, the lamp should be raised as the bird improves. Better still is to mount the lamp to one side, so that the patient can move away to the other end of the cage out of the heat.

The recovered grey was subsequently paired up with a hen in an outside aviary, and – like most African grey parrots – the pair spent most of their time in their nest box, and were not seen from one day to the next by their keeper. He assumed they were well, as food and water

African grey parrot with an advanced squamous cell carcinoma (skin cancer) on his head, following earlier burning of the skin in this area by prolonged exposure to an infra-red lamp.

were being consumed, but he did not check. Ultimately, the cock bird did show itself, by which time he was unable to hold his head upright, and the crown of his head carried a huge crusty growth. This growth turned out to be an advanced skin cancer, which had penetrated the bird's skull to the brain beneath. It was obviously inoperable and incurable, and the parrot died. So the third lesson is to maintain that vigil; continue to observe your birds; and do not just assume that they are healthy!

quarantining new arrivals, as mentioned above, and not mixing new birds immediately with existing stock. Good hygiene and regular disinfection of food and water bowls, perches, nest boxes, toys and cages are essential. The control of vermin and the secure storage of good-quality food in airtight containers are important. Selection of sound, healthy stock in the first place is obviously wise;

and the feeding of a top quality, well-balanced diet, suited to the species is paramount. Finally, regular observation of your birds, to identify subtle changes in their normal behaviour and attitude, will enable you to spot problems before they become too advanced.

If you do consider that you have a sick bird, then there are three useful things to do.

- The first is isolation. Separate the bird from any companions, and bring it into a small indoor cage. This will allow you more closely to observe it and monitor its progress; more easily to administer any medication that may be required; hopefully to avoid further spread of the disease should it be contagious; and to avoid bullying of the sick bird by other members of its group.
- Secondly warmth. Birds have a high metabolic rate, and will expend a lot of energy just to maintain their body temperature. Supplying external warmth will aid the bird's recovery by enabling it to divert energy to getting better. This may simply mean bringing an aviary bird indoors. Alternatively, use a heat pad, a hot-water bottle, an airing cupboard, or place the cage near a radiator. It may be worth investing in a hospital cage, or an infra-red heat lamp.
- The third important home therapy is fluids. Sick birds will dehydrate rapidly, especially if they have vomiting or diarrhoea. Encouraging their fluid intake by sweetening their drinking water with honey, sugar, glucose, or fruit juices will prove invaluable. Better still are proprietary oral electrolyte solutions. If the parrot will not drink voluntarily, these must be administered by spoon, dropper, syringe, or crop tube.

If your bird is ill, resist the temptation to reach for the old pot of antibiotic powder at the back of the cupboard, or worse still to use some prescribed for a friend's birds. As I hope by now I have made clear, antibiotics are effective only against bacterial infections, which account for only about 25 per cent of sick birds. You will do far better to give a probiotic, as well as the fluids and electrolytes, until you have obtained a proper diagnosis. This will have the effect of boosting your bird's immune system and aiding its digestion, while it recovers.

DISEASES ASSOCIATED WITH THE BREEDING OF PARROTS
Neonatal (Paediatric) Diseases

Dead in Shell

Embryos dying during incubation are most commonly the result of problems with temperature and humidity. Therefore careful monitoring of the incubator is paramount. Chilling of the egg will suspend the development of the embryo, and prolonged periods of cold will kill it. Excess heat will dehydrate it, as will insufficient humidity; while humidity that is too high will result in a water-logged egg and drowning of the embryo. Occasionally, infectious agents may get into the egg, and sometimes there are genetic or toxic factors involved. The cause of early embryonic death may be investigated by an experienced veterinarian or laboratory, but the egg has to be fresh (within a few hours) since secondary bacterial contaminants will quickly grow in the egg and mask the true problem.

Problems at Hatching

Death at hatching is commonly the result of dehydration because humidity is not high enough during the hatching period. Shell membranes dry out and the shell becomes hard, while the chick gets stuck to its membranes and weakens.

Citron-crested cockatoo chick – strong, calling for food, with healthy new feathers and light pink skin.

Humidity at this time needs to be around 70 per cent, and drops of water may be applied to the chick's beak tip as it works at the crack in the shell.

Alternatively, there may be too much interference on the part of the bird-keeper, leading to haemorrhage in the egg or the introduction of infection. Mal-positioning results from dehydration or insufficient turning of the egg during incubation, so that again the chick will stick to shell membranes and be unable to manoeuvre. Omphalitis, or yolk sac infection, results from a delay of the sac to be absorbed, premature hatching, or too much handling of the chick. Deformity or stunting of chicks can result from incubation temperatures that are too high, poor nutrition of the parents, or genetic influences.

Healthy chicks should be alert and beg in response to sound or movement. The skin should be smooth and pale pink. Babies that are dehydrated will appear grey and wrinkled, while those that have septicaemia will be dark red and wrinkled. Both will be sleepy and inactive.

Chicks and Juveniles

Several viruses affect parrot chicks (see above for full details of these infections). The most important are polyomavirus and psittacine beak and

Feathers from a cockatoo affected with PBFD virus, on the left. They are short, deformed, and 'pinched' compared with the normal two feathers on the right.

feather disease (PBFD). The former will cause rapid death in young chicks, showing a very pale skin colour, with small spots of haemorrhage. PBFD generally affects slightly older chicks, as they start to grow feathers. The new feathers will be clubbed or constricted, and will fall out easily. Birds will die with acute organ failure or secondary infection as their immune systems are severely damaged.

Proventricular dilatation disease (PDD) will affect weaning birds, resulting in death following a distended stomach, weight loss, vomiting, diarrhoea with undigested food particles, and nervous signs. Being infectious diseases, these conditions are most commonly a problem in large nurseries, especially where chicks are obtained from several sources. Thus having a closed, limited population, or an 'all-in, all-out' policy, with good hygiene practice and fumigation of the premises between batches, will go a long way towards controlling such infections.

Red urine is seen particularly in juvenile African grey parrots, and occasionally Pionus and Amazons, and is not a cause for alarm. It appears to be a reaction between ingredients in the feeding formula with chemicals (possibly bleach) in paper towelling. A change of food or bedding and the colour will disappear.

Mouth and throat infections are common in baby parrots, and will follow poor feeding techniques, contaminated food, or physical damage from parent birds, siblings in the nest, or the hand-feeding utensils. The infectious agents may be either bacteria or yeasts, so swabs from the mouth should be cultured and examined to identify the agent. Bacteria will require antibiotic treatment; yeasts will need anti-fungal drugs such as nystatin.

Crop problems are common in chicks. They include puncture by the feeding tube, especially if not using one with a rounded tip, and occur especially in strong-pumping feeders like macaws. The hole would require surgical repair. Foreign bodies include portions (or even the whole length!) of rubber feeding tubes swallowed by the chick, but most frequently the problem would be wood shaving or chips used as a nesting material. Small pieces will be softened, partially digested, and will eventually pass through, but larger fragments will lodge in the crop or stomach and will prevent food going down. If quickly identified, fresh fragments may be massaged back up through the mouth. Otherwise a very liquid diet, with some lubrication like liquid paraffin or corn oil will encourage passage of the material. Extreme cases may require surgical removal.

DOWN THE HATCH

One client who rears quite a few parrots had a young Black-headed caique that swallowed a whole peanut kernel while sitting with a group of older chicks. The breeder was concerned that the nut would cause a problem, so I advised her to try to 'milk it' back up out of the crop. She did not have enough confidence to do this comfortably, so brought the bird to me. A little gentle, sustained massage of the nut up the chick's neck, over the tongue, and out it popped!

Crop stasis is a frequent problem. Food material accumulates in this organ, and may rapidly ferment and develop secondary infections – 'sour crop'. Reasons would include hypothermia, dehydration, foreign bodies, or infections. Large volumes of liquid content need to be massaged out, with the chick turned upside down so that it does not choke in the process. This should be followed by small, frequent, very liquid meals. It helps to slightly acidify the formula by adding a few drops of lemon juice or apple cider vinegar. Swabs from the crop content should be taken to check for bacteria or yeasts, and antibiotic or anti-fungal treatment given if required.

Occasionally, the crop may become seriously over-distended, so that it sags down over the chest and cannot empty because the contents are below the oesophageal exit. These may be treated with a 'crop bra' of soft tape wrapped around the lower neck and chest, to lift up the crop, at the same time feeding small, frequent meals.

Crop burns are a serious complication of feeding food that is too hot. This is easily done if formula

African grey chick recovering from surgery to repair a 'crop burn'. There was a hole in his neck leaking food after formula had been fed too hot, resulting in a perforating ulcer through the crop wall.

is heated in a microwave oven and not thoroughly stirred. 'Hot spots' in the mix will scald the sensitive inner lining of the crop, leading to localized inflammation, ulceration, and secondary infection. The chick will be become dull and reluctant to feed, and after several days the ulceration may break through the crop wall and the overlying skin. Often the first sign noticed by the keeper is food dribbling out of a hole in the bird's neck! This damage requires surgical repair, but the veterinarian will need to wait until the burned tissue has showed its full extent. Suturing the wound too early will result in breakdown as more flesh dies back and the stitches pull out. All dead tissue will need to be removed, and healthy crop wall sutured together, with the skin similarly repaired in a separate layer.

Budgerigar chick showing 'splayed legs'. The legs are spread sideways owing to deformity at the hip and knee joints, resulting from lack of calcium.

Cockatiel chick with its head feathers plucked by its parents who wanted to go down to breed again. Note the clearly visible ear opening, which is usually covered with feathers.

Injuries may be inflicted by parent birds due to inexperience, disturbance or a desire to breed again. This may be as mild as a little feather plucking over the head and neck, but can include the removal of toes, wing tips, or even beaks.

Young Jardine's parrot (Poicephalus gulielmi) *with its upper beak (rostrum) torn away by its parent birds. Once properly removed and cauterized, this beak will slowly re-grow over the next several months, and the bird will manage to eat a soft-food diet.*

Skeletal problems are also common in parrot chicks. Most frequently encountered is Metabolic Bone Disease (MBD), commonly known as 'rickets', and is the result of nutritional imbalance – usually a lack of calcium and vitamin D, with too much phosphorus in the diet fed to the parent birds (*see* Chapter 6). African grey and Eclectus parrots seem particularly susceptible. Affected chicks will show splayed legs or folding fractures of the long bones of the legs and wings. If caught early enough, splayed legs may be hobbled

The same bird after two weeks. The tissue is healing well, and the bird is managing soft food successfully.

My grey parrot Eric as a chick, showing a full crop and a bowing deformity of his right leg. He had a greenstick fracture just above the angle joint that had healed, but at a right-angle to the normal line.

A young grey parrot in a pet store with dropped wings, because of a bowing deformity of the humerus (bone between shoulder and elbow) resulting from calcium deficiency.

together with soft tape. Fractures in soft, rapidly growing bones may be strapped and splinted, and will heal quickly if calcium supplements are added to the diet. The affected chicks will need support with crumpled paper in the nest container to keep the legs together. More advanced cases may need to have the deformed bone broken and re-set surgically when the bird is mature enough to withstand such an operation. Skeletal injuries of this type may be exacerbated by careless restraint of the chicks when hand-feeding, or by over-activity of the growing heavy chick on soft, weakened bones.

Constricted toes are found in African grey and Eclectus parrots as well as large macaws. The affected digit will appear swollen distal to an apparent tight annular fibrous band. Some cases may be

A closer view of the right-angle bend in the leg, above the foot.

Scarlet macaw (Ara macao) *showing 'scissor beak' – the upper beak (rostrum) is deviated to the bird's right side. A metal brace had been fitted above the upper jaw, with braided wire attached to the tip of the rostrum to draw it back into position. This wire had broken, and was about to be replaced.*

The wire brace replaced and padded. This 'orthodontic' apparatus needs to stay in place for about six weeks until the beak alignment is improved.

the result of fibrous nest material wrapped around the toe, but most have fibrous scab. Either way, the fibre or scab material needs to be removed with a fine-pointed scalpel blade or pointed scissors. Soaking the toe in warm water may help, but if not caught early enough the tip of the toe may develop dry gangrene and eventually drop off. Dehydration is believed to be a partial cause of this problem.

Beak deformities include an undershot jaw (mandibular prognathism), where the lower mandible extends beyond the upper rostrum, and is particularly seen in cockatoos. If recognized early it may be corrected by calcium supplementation and manipulation of the soft beak tissue while feeding. More established deformities may require corrective orthodontic surgery. Scissor beak is found in macaws, and is a lateral deviation resulting from congenital abnormalities, dietary deficiencies, or clumsy feeding techniques. Correction may be achieved by using a surgical brace.

Adult Female Problems

Hen parrots suffer from many egg-related conditions, which include no eggs or soft-shelled eggs. The former may simply be because the hen is immature, but both will result from poor diet and calcium deficiency problems.

A soft-shelled egg. The hen bird has mobilized sufficient calcium to part-produce the shell, but then has run out of reserves before the shell has completed its full hard layers.

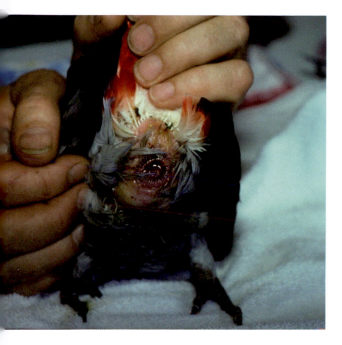

Prolapsed oviduct in a Timneh grey. The swollen lining of the cloaca (vent) has turned inside out and will need to be replaced under anaesthetic, and possibly sutured back in position.

African grey parrot having difficulty expelling her egg. At this stage of the process, an injection of calcium, lubrication and gentle manipulation will generally produce the egg.

Egg-binding occurs when the hen has an egg in the lower oviduct and cloaca that she cannot deliver. This also results from inadequate calcium – this mineral is needed not only to form the eggshell, but also for proper muscle contraction. Cold, damp conditions will also affect proper delivery. Most cases will respond to warmth, fluids and calcium. Some birds will require gentle massage of the egg, with lubrication, to manoeuvre it down the oviduct, but such handling should be performed with care as the increased abdominal pressure can compromise the bird's breathing. Extreme cases may need to have the egg collapsed by sucking out its contents with a needle; or else surgery may be necessary to remove the egg from the oviduct. In these circumstances it is important to ensure that no eggshell fragments remain.

Some prolific layers will prolapse their oviduct or cloacal lining, and this will require professional surgical repair and replacement. Many hens will suffer a partial paralysis of one or both legs after producing a large egg. This again may be linked to calcium deficiency but also to bruising. It is usually temporary, and will respond to therapy with calcium and anti-inflammatory drugs plus soft support for the body.

Over-production of eggs is encountered in budgerigars, lovebirds, and especially cockatiels, which tend to be prolific breeders. This is controlled by reducing the photoperiod (daylight length) by closing curtains or covering the cage; by removing toys and mirrors that may stimulate breeding behaviour; and by not handling or stroking the bird excessively over its rump or under the wings, since this activity will stimulate breeding behaviour. Eggs that are laid should not be removed, since this will simply encourage the hen to lay more to replace them, and this will tire her out and deplete her calcium reserves. Three or four eggs should be left with her. Even a single hen may sit on this clutch and attempt to incubate them, but as the eggs are infertile obviously nothing will happen. The hen eventually will realize that there is no activity inside the eggs, and will lose interest and come away from them. That is the time to remove them from her, but at least her system has had time to rest and recover from the process. Really severe and persistent cases may require hormone therapy or even surgical removal of the oviduct (salpingectomy) – the equivalent of a hysterectomy in a mammal.

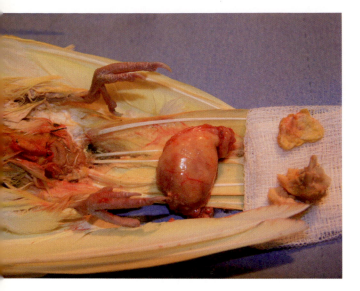

A portion of the oviduct, with retained egg material, removed from a cockatiel (Nymphicus hollandicus).

Inspissated eggs. The egg material is laid down in concentric layers inside the bird, its cut surface giving the appearance of an onion.

Egg-peritonitis and retained dried inspissated eggs are extremely common in poultry, but will occur in parrots, notably cockatiels. Peritonitis follows leakage of egg material into the abdominal cavity, resulting in an inflammatory response, secondary infection, swelling and fluid accumulation. This may be fatal if not treated, and will require at least flushing and cleaning of the abdominal cavity, or even salpingectomy. Inspissated eggs are concentric layers of yolk material impacted on each other and drying out, forming a firm mass within the oviduct. This condition would also require surgical correction.

Tumours and cysts involving the ovary may also be found in adult hens. These will manifest as irregular egg-laying, abdominal swelling, colour change of the cere in the budgerigar, or lameness resulting from the pressure of the enlarged tissue on the pelvic nerves.

Adult Male Problems

Masturbation is a frequent behavioural problem in pet parrots. These are usually single pet birds, strongly bonded to the owner, and stimulated by the owner's incessant stroking of the rump and under the wings. Cockatoos, cockatiels and budgerigars are the prime culprits. Persistent masturbation will lead to cloacal soreness and even prolapse.

Engorged and prolapsed cloacal tissue from Moluccan cockatoo Aristo. This severely frustrated bird was a persistent masturbator, and required prolonged hormone treatment and behavioural therapy, as well as several surgical repairs to contain the prolapse.

CASE STUDY

Charlie was a normal grey young male cockatiel owned as a much-loved pet by a little old lady living on her own. Like all male grey cockatiels, he had the distinctive brightly coloured yellow head with orange cheek patches, and his under tail coverts were plain grey. Hen birds are duller in the head colouring, and have yellow striations under the tail.

The owner became concerned when Charlie started persistently to rub his vent on his perch, and make funny little squeaking noises as he did so, so she took him to a local domestic pet veterinary practice. The vet suspected constipation and prescribed liquid paraffin, and Charlie passed some very oily droppings over the next few days, but still continued with its upsetting behaviour.

Charlie's owner was still worried, so she took him back to the clinic and saw a different vet, who thought the bird might be egg-bound. Now we have established that these birds are sexually dimorphic (*see* Chapter 3), and he was therefore identifiable as a cock bird if the vet had known that simple fact. However, this was not recognized, so Charlie was admitted for X-ray examination. Unsurprisingly there was no sign of an egg on the radiograph, but the veterinarian still thought there may be some egg-related problem, and gave an injection of calcium. Now that would have been helpful had there been some egg retention, but Charlie returned home and continued his rubbing and squeaking.

His owner eventually obtained my details and came to see me as a veterinarian experienced in avian problems. After a little discussion and a simple examination, I was able to reassure his owner that Charlie was a perfectly healthy young male, and that he was just doing what all little boys do at adolescence!

Charlie, a young adult normal Grey cockatiel that worried his owner with his repeated adolescent sexual behaviour.

The owner was very relieved, and Charlie was obviously quite happy, but he had been put through unnecessary procedures and his owner had incurred unnecessary expense, simply because of the lack of recognition by the vets of normal parrot behaviour.

Cloacal papilloma in a Green-winged macaw (Ara chloroptera). *This is a virus-induced wart that will enlarge inside the vent, causing straining to pass droppings, local bleeding, and difficulty in mating and breeding.*

Hawk-headed parrot (Deroptyus accipitrinus). *This is another species particularly susceptible to virus papillomata. Note the attractive blue and red head feathers, that may be raised at will in a 'frill' around the bird's head in fear, aggression, or excitement.*

Aggression is also linked with testosterone-production in adolescent or adult males. Natural territorial defence and displays will occur between rival breeding males in aviary collections, but such sexual aggression can become a problem when it occurs in the indoor pet bird. Very often it is the hand-reared parrot that has no fear of humans that can be the most troublesome, with cockatoos and some Amazons being the worst culprits. Management is by behavioural training techniques described in Chapter 10, or in some cases hormone therapy can be very effective.

Infertility can be a problem in birds intended for breeding. It may simply be the result of immaturity and inexperience, in which case the parrot will learn in time, and especially if he is placed with an older hen or is able to observe other birds. Poor diet will have an influence, so proper nutrition needs to be addressed, with possible supplements, especially those containing vitamin E. Physical problems may make the act of mating difficult, including leg or foot injuries, deformities, arthritis or obesity. Another cause may be cloacal papillomata, which are virus-induced warts especially common in green-winged macaws, some Amazons, and hawk-headed parrots *(Deroptyus accipitrinus)*. These will grow just inside, and protrude from, the cloaca (vent) of both sexes, and provide a physical barrier to successful mating.

Cock birds will also get tumours of their testes; again budgerigars are the most frequently affected species. As with the hens, the resultant organ swelling will press against the pelvic nerves, causing partial leg paralysis, loss of bodyweight, and usually a distended abdomen. Abnormal hormones produced by the tumour may produce a colour change from blue to brown in a budgie's cere, or behavioural changes in all birds.

CHAPTER 9

Grooming and Feather Plucking

In this book you will have noticed many pictures of parrots with less than perfect plumage. We established in Chapter 1 that feathers are unique to birds, and in parrots particularly the combination of colours and feather patterns is what attracts people to keep them. Thus the slightest upset to the 'feather-perfect' picture is of immediate concern to the owner, and will prompt them to seek advice – probably more readily than more subtle changes in bodyweight, appetite, or behaviour. Feather-plucking is a common problem in captive parrots, and causes many headaches to client and veterinarian alike in attempting to stop it, and therefore warrants considerable exploration. Firstly, however, I should like briefly to deal with nail, beak, and wing clipping.

Orange-winged Amazon with an injured mandible that now grows with an abnormal curvature and requires regular trimming.

GROOMING

(This section applies largely to indoor pet parrots rather than aviary collections.)

Beaks may become injured or mal-aligned, and then will need regular clipping and/or grinding to maintain their shape. Those that become excessively overgrown or flaky generally do so because of underlying disease problems such as liver disease, psittacine beak and feather disease, or mite infestation, so such cases should always be investigated further. The beak grows in layers and it is natural for these layers to flake off from the outside

Leadbeater's cockatoo with a similar injury. In both birds, part of the mandible was bitten off by their partners.

Slender-billed conure – a species with a naturally long rostral beak – this does not need to be clipped! (Photo: Tony Pittman)

surface, but excessive flaking may indicate dietary deficiencies or liver disease. Remember also that some birds have naturally long upper beaks that do not require clipping!

Claws may become overgrown in pet parrots and require clipping or grinding, but once again excessively overgrown or deformed claws may be indicative of poor diet or liver disease. Pedicure perches will help to keep the claws in trim. In many cases, the parrot's claws have their sharp tips removed more for the owner's benefit, as they find it uncomfortable to have the parrot climbing over their bare skin with sharp claws. (See also page 36.)

Wing-Clipping

Wing-clipping is a far more controversial issue. Many pet-stores and bird dealers will carry out wing clips for their customers, as will veterinarians not regularly treating birds. However, the technique is still often improperly or poorly performed, and is the subject of much controversy even among avian veterinarians. There are so many methods of clipping recommended or described, many of which are useless or even damaging.

Many people believe that parrots should never be wing-clipped: they were made to fly, and clipping somehow affects their mental state. However, in the pet bird situation, where a parrot is a family member and is allowed freedom in the household, the power of free flight can be a positive disadvantage, and even a hazard to the bird. Fully flighted birds will get into areas where owners may not want them; they may damage ornaments and decorations; they may reach materials which can be chewed, such as door and window frames; they may fly into fires or cooking pans; and in the summer they may escape through open doors and windows.

We also encounter mate aggression in paired birds, where one enthusiastic partner (usually the cock bird) in the breeding season can continually chase its mate, who may not yet be in breeding condition. This will result in fatigue and loss of condition in the chased bird: very often feathers are damaged, or the bird will not be allowed to feed or will be physically attacked. Clipping the wing of the aggressive partner will reduce such harassment, and will allow the mate to recover while she comes into breeding condition. In all other circumstances, paired birds living in aviaries should be allowed free flight.

It is in theory a simple operation to cut some feathers so that the bird cannot fly, but the correct method requires some knowledge of feather anatomy and the different flying abilities of various species. *There is no one technique that can be applied to all birds.*

The Technique

The aim of the procedure is to allow the bird controlled downward flight, with no possibility of lift.

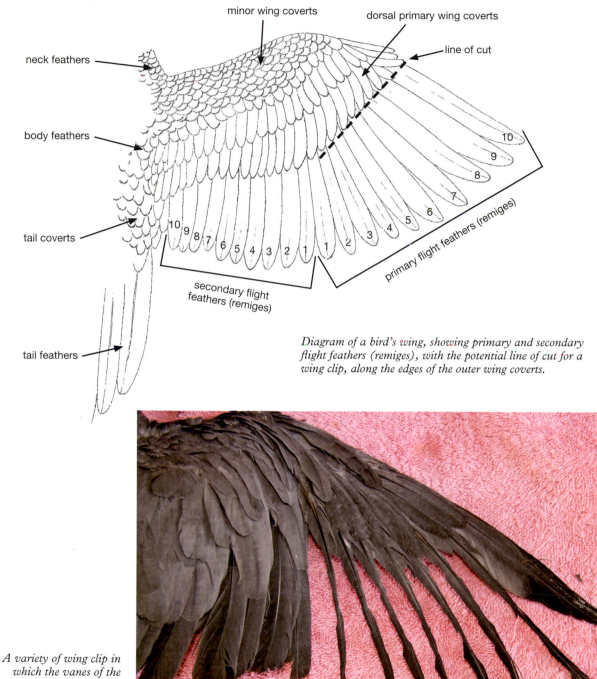

neck feathers

body feathers

tail coverts

tail feathers

minor wing coverts

dorsal primary wing coverts

line of cut

10
9
8
7
6
5
4
3
2
1

primary flight feathers (remiges)

10 9 8 7 6 5 4 3 2 1

secondary flight feathers (remiges)

Diagram of a bird's wing, showing primary and secondary flight feathers (remiges), with the potential line of cut for a wing clip, along the edges of the outer wing coverts.

A variety of wing clip in which the vanes of the feathers are removed by cutting lengthwise along the shaft. While this will prevent flight, it will also give the bird something to worry at and play with, potentially leading to feather destruction.

The bird should not fall heavily to the ground: this will often result in injury to legs or sternum. The method chosen must achieve this objective while at the same time satisfying the aesthetic requirements of the owner.

It is important for the clipper to discuss first with the owner the various options, and to indicate to them that wing clipping provides only temporary control of flight. Many owners do not realize that once the bird moults and loses the cut feathers and grows new ones, it will fly again. They therefore need to be prepared to return to have the procedure repeated on a regular basis: the frequency will depend on the species and the stage of the moult at the time of the clipping.

The bird will need to be restrained comfortably, preferably with the aid of a competent assistant or technician. A towel should be used for the larger parrots, while a cockatiel or smaller bird may be held in the bare hand. It is never advisable to allow the bird owner to hold their pet for this procedure: most are unable adequately to restrain the bird safely; many are tense and therefore in danger of holding the bird too tightly; plus the fact that the bird will then associate the experience with its owner, and may lose its trust in that owner.

The wing to be clipped should be gently but firmly extended, holding it over the radius/ulna. The selected feathers may then be cut. I have seen many suggestions by various bird-keepers as to which feathers should be cut and how. Some operatives have suggested cutting alternate flight feathers to retain some appearance of normality. This will not work – the bird will still fly. Parrots lose feathers in the wings as they moult, yet will still fly. An alternative suggestion is to cut along the length of the shaft, removing the barbs, but retaining the quill. My response to this technique is to ask why? This simply leaves exposed shafts that will inevitably irritate the bird, and lead to feather mutilation.

The preferred method is to cut primary feathers along the line of the external wing coverts. This reference point is significant: to cut at a level lower than this line will allow the bird still to fly. Whilst the feather cut may be tidied up to just under the covert line, it is important not to take the cut too high. Note that the external wing coverts extend further than the internal feathers. If

Wing of an Amazon parrot, showing the completed cut. The outer two primary feathers (9 and 10) have been left intact to protect the leading edge of the wing, and for cosmetic reasons. The wing looks tidier when at rest.

these are used as a reference, the trim will be too high. This can result in two problems: the first is that new growing feathers, still encased in their protective sheaths (blood feathers) may be cut, with resulting haemorrhage. The shorter cut will also mean that the quills left may create a problem at the next moult, similar to the situation found when recently trapped birds taken for importation are savagely and carelessly hacked by the native trappers to prevent them flying. These over-short feathers become a source of irritation to the bird, and in many cases will lead to feather plucking. It is my opinion also that the natural moulting process depends in part on the weight of the old feather pulling at the follicle and gradually working loose. If the feather stump is too short, then this weight stimulus is not present, and the feathers are not lost at the proper interval. I have seen birds damaged in this way, still carrying these short quills eighteen months after importation.

The next – and most important – dilemma is how many feathers should be cut? The answer has to be variable, according to the species involved. Light-bodied, long-winged strong-flying birds like cockatiels will require more feathers to be removed than will a stocky, short-winged species such as an

Wing of a grey parrot with all the primary flight feathers clipped.

New blood feathers on a heavily clipped wing. The unprotected leading edge has become damaged, and the soft new feathers are very vulnerable to breaking and haemorrhage.

Amazon parrot. Each patient has to be treated individually, and the required effect discussed with the owner. An obese pet Amazon may require only four or five feathers removed. My preference is to retain the outer primary feathers (9 and 10) for cosmetic effect when the wings are in their resting position crossed over the body. This is controversial, with many veterinarians suggesting that this leaves these outer feathers vulnerable to injury. When dealing with the strong fliers, it is essential to take seven to ten feathers, including the outer flights 9 and 10.

After the clip is performed, the bird should be tested to ensure that the desired effect is achieved. If not, more feathers may be cut, after consultation with the owner to confirm the required degree of flight control. There is also discussion among veterinarians as to whether one or both wings should be clipped. The general feeling and current practice is that both wings should be cut to avoid the 'spiralling' effect of clipping just one side.

Clipping the secondary flight feathers certainly will not prevent flight – yet I have seen many birds clipped in this fashion by pet-store workers or inexperienced veterinarians. Owners naturally become upset when their birds still fly around their heads, or worse still, escape! I have also seen clips where all primaries and secondaries have been removed. This is excessive and unnecessary.

Frequency of Clipping

As mentioned earlier, we have to consider the natural lifestyle of the bird: worn-out feathers are regularly replaced in the process known as moulting. In the majority of birds (including parrots)

Wing with the secondary flight feathers clipped. The primaries are still intact, so the bird will still fly!

this replacement process is sequential. It therefore follows that wing-clipping is a temporary process, with the cut feathers gradually being replaced by new growth. The interval between rendering a bird flightless, and the return of aerobatic ability, will depend on the stage of the moult at which the clip was performed. If the patient has recently moulted at this time, then it will be six to nine months before new growth takes place. Conversely, if the bird is due to moult when clipped, then new feather growth will occur within a few weeks. It will take only two or three replacement feathers in strong flying species for flight to be possible. The owners must be advised of this, and should expect to have the bird trimmed again soon.

Age at First Clipping

Once again, considering the everyday nature and apparent simplicity of this procedure, there is conflicting opinion as to the age at which a pet bird should first be clipped. Many bird dealers and pet shops will routinely clip a young bird at point of sale so that the new owners have no problems with their new pet flying around the house and causing havoc. There is also the opinion that such restraint of the new pet will make the taming process easier, and that clipping a young bird at this age is akin to nail clipping or grooming a puppy, with the expectation that the animal will become accustomed to the procedure, and will not resent it in later life.

The converse opinion is that a young bird should first be allowed to develop the physical ability to fly, and to learn how to control that ability properly, before it is taken away. This means that the pectoral musculature becomes fully developed. African grey parrots particularly seem to require a learning process for flying; otherwise they lack co-ordination and control, resulting in physical injury to themselves and their environment. My feeling is that this initial learning and developing process is important, and therefore wing clipping should not be carried out in too young a bird.

The foregoing is intended to put forward the advantages and disadvantages of what seems on the face of it to be a simple technique. There are very many bad wing clips performed by inexperienced operatives, or those who do not understand the mechanics of birds' flight. These cases have brought the technique a bad name, but I maintain that there is a place in pet birds for a good wing clip, properly performed.

I accept that the majority of birds are just built to fly, and there is no greater sight than watching these magnificent creatures soaring, hovering, swooping, gliding, and flapping in their natural environment. However, if we accept the premise that we are going to keep such creatures in captivity (and that in itself is controversial to many people!), then we must also accept that this modification of their lifestyle brings with it many changes. If wing clipping can make that lifestyle safer and allow greater freedom for the pet bird, then my contention is – provided it is carried out properly and efficiently – that this technique has a valid place in pet bird husbandry.

FEATHER PLUCKING

Just as with any general disease problem in birds, a few displayed symptoms can represent a whole range of causes of the illness, so it follows that there are many reasons why a bird's feathers may become damaged or lost. These would include inherited defects, dietary deficiencies, infections, and physical damage from the environment or other birds.

To the inexperienced eye, one damaged feather looks much like another, whereas experience and more detailed analysis will hopefully identify the alternative causes. Thus skilful diagnosis is required to establish the cause and thereby to suggest a possible cure; but there is no more frustrating condition for the disappointed owner and the veterinarian attempting to treat the bird than the feather plucker.

The first point to note is that *feather plucking is a disease of captivity* – it does not occur (except as natural physiological behaviour in breeding birds) in wild-living individuals. Many owners appear to give their birds the best of care and attention, and yet are rewarded by a bird that rips out all its feathers; whilst other individuals can live in apparently appalling environments and still have immaculate plumage.

Rainbow lory showing multi-coloured, patterned feathering – part of what attracts people to keeping parrots.

Secondly it is important to realize from the outset that no case of feather plucking will respond to a miraculous overnight cure, nor can the answer be given in a two-minute consultation. There is no universal panacea: what will solve the problem in one bird may have no effect in another individual, because of the different root cause.

Diagnosis

In attempting to investigate a feather-plucking problem, one has to be able to recognize the normal from the abnormal, and to eliminate all other possible causes of feather disease. Thus a proper clinical diagnosis is required, just as with any other disease. The process follows that described in Chapter 8, and will include detailed questioning of the owner as to the background of the bird – where it came from, where it is kept, how it is fed, when the problem started and how the problem is manifest.

Examination of the environment is important – the presence of parasites or irritants may be detected, plus one can get a general impression of the bird's lifestyle. The bird will then need a thorough examination, probably linked to laboratory tests such as blood samples to assess liver and kidney function and hormone levels; or to check for infectious agents such as psittacine beak and feather disease (PBFD). It may be necessary to examine feather samples or skin biopsies for the presence of bacteria, viruses, fungi, or parasites.

It is perfectly normal for a bird to pluck the head and neck feathers of its mate in the breeding season, or for parents to over-preen their chicks in the same way. It is also normal for birds to lose feathers over the breast area while breeding (the brood patch), but both these may be triggers to start a bird on the road to longer term plucking. New feathers that grow in the normal moult will irritate as they come through, and birds will preen heavily at this time, but again the scales can tip easily from preening to plucking if the irritation is excessive. This would be the case when many feathers are replaced at once, for example following accident or illness. But then a vicious circle is established, because the large number of growing feathers irritates; this leads to plucking, which means more feathers are grown to replace those pulled out, which means more irritation, and therefore more picking, and so on.

Certain internal or systemic disease conditions will produce skin irritation that results in plucking. Liver disease is one; giardiasis in cockatiels is another. This protozoal intestinal infection is well documented as being a cause of feather picking in the USA, although we tend not to see so much in the UK. The remedy in these cases is obviously to treat the underlying disease rather than simply to try to control the picking.

Dietary problems are also highly significant in feather disease. Still far too many caged birds are kept on an inadequate or imbalanced diet, and deficiencies of vitamins (especially A), minerals (especially calcium), trace elements (such as zinc), and amino acids will result in poor feather and skin quality, which in turn predispose to plucking. In some cases too much of a dietary component can cause a problem – a fat-rich diet, or simple obesity, will produce poor feather quality. This subject has been covered thoroughly in Chapters 6 and 8.

The bird's environment is extremely important: smoke in the atmosphere, or fat droplets where a bird is kept near a pub kitchen for example, will be deposited on the feathers and will cause irritation. Handling a bird with nicotine-stained fingers after smoking will irritate a bird's skin, and will start the bird pecking to relieve the itch. A dry, dusty atmosphere is very bad for plumage quality – the feathers will become brittle and will then irritate. Regular bathing or spraying is essential. Lighting is important – too long a photoperiod (length of daylight) may tire the bird, or stimulate breeding activity, or encourage frequent moulting. Light levels that are too low will result in poor quality feather growth.

Another environmental consideration is boredom. This is frequently cited as a cause of feather plucking, but in my experience it is by no means the commonest cause. Parrots are extremely

Dermatitis on the feet of an Amazon parrot. One possible cause of this condition is handling of the bird with nicotine-stained fingers, as the nicotine will irritate the bird's skin.

A very old Scarlet macaw, showing pigmented spots in the iris of its eye, a chronic groove in the beak from a persistent nasal discharge, and retained feather-sheaths on its head owing to an inability to preen itself because of arthritis.

intelligent creatures, and do need a lot of physical and mental stimulation to satisfy their needs. Therefore toys, objects to chew, radios playing, playtime with the owner, are all important for their well-being, and in many cases the provision of such diversions where they are not present will prevent plucking in a bird. However, the opposite situation can also apply – that is to say that a bird's environment can be too busy. In an active household, with children playing and running around, dogs barking, music blaring, and general busy-ness from dawn until way past dusk, the poor bird may get over-stimulated and have no chance of proper rest. This can result in feather pulling, and the answer in this case is obviously to move the bird to a more relaxed atmosphere.

In some cases there may be an inability to preen. The feathers will then look untidy, with persistent sheaths, and possibly secondarily infected, but they will not be plucked out. This could be the case in a hand-reared bird that has not been socialized with others, and has never really learned how to preen; or it may result from some damage to the beak that prevents grooming activity. A further option is arthritis in an older bird, reducing its flexibility to reach certain areas of its plumage.

Specific infections of the skin or feathers may lead to plucking because of the resultant irritation. These would include bacterial infections of the skin (dermatitis) or feather follicles (folliculitis); fungal diseases (similar to conditions such as athlete's foot, or ringworm); or virus infections such as PBFD or Polyomavirus.

Parasitic infestations by such creatures as mites, lice, or ticks, are commonly suspected as causes of feather picking, and many cans of mite spray are sold in consequence. In fact, single pet birds are unlikely to be afflicted in this way, unless they have come recently from a collection. Small aviary and colony birds, such as parakeets and budgerigars may occasionally be affected by such organisms. One other parasitic condition that is quite common as a cause of skin disease (although rarely feather plucking) is the mange mite Cnemidocoptes (*see* Chapter 8).

Thus to diagnose and treat a case of feather plucking, one has to consider and eliminate or test for all of the above.

Adolescent Problems

Plucking often starts at adolescence, or following some episode of stress. The time of day that plucking occurs is significant. 'Situation' plucking in response to something that annoys the bird is common: for example, being put away at night when he doesn't want to go! Birds are very sensitive to environment and routine – *see* case history box in Chapter 8. Jealousy and stress are commonly implicated – having builders in or relatives to stay; holiday times or other changes in routine may all be responsible for starting a bird pulling at its feathers.

The area of feathers that the bird attacks is also significant. Hormone changes and broody behaviour most commonly influence chest and shoulder pluckers, while a small local area may indicate some underlying internal pain.

In my experience, most cases of plucking that are not the result of one of the disease processes listed above occur in adolescent birds. Hand-reared African grey parrots are perhaps the worst offenders, but Eclectus and cockatoos come close. Although birds have been kept in captivity for some generations, they are still far from being domesticated species like the dog and cat. The artificial incubation and hand rearing of parrots is

Male Eclectus parrot Chocky – a chronic plucker who persistently chews his wing and tail feathers, resulting in this scruffy appearance.

Dougal yet again, illustrating distinctive features of a self-plucker: his body feathers have been removed, while his head and crest feathers are intact since he cannot reach them. Nevertheless, it is possible for some parrots to damage their head feathers using their claws, or by rubbing their heads against a perch or cage bars.

a much more recent phenomenon, and these birds grow up not really sure whether they are bird or human! When they reach those 'awkward teenage years', and their hormones tell them they need to breed, they are not quite sure which way to turn, and hence start plucking in frustration and confusion. It is also possible that the hormone changes cause direct irritability of the skin, just as in human teenagers with acne. A commonly suggested solution in such cases is to 'get the bird a mate', but this is not always the answer. A companion bird of a different species may help, but a true opposite sex of the same species may throw the bird into even more confusion. They may even copy each other, and you end up with two plucked birds!

So What's to Be Done?

So having identified our bird as a plucker, and confirmed by the above examinations and analysis that it is not suffering from a specific disease, what can we do about it? I hope I have demonstrated that the causes can be so varied that no one single treatment could possibly work for every bird, but there are some general suggestions that I offer as background therapy in every case.

- *Regular spraying or bathing with warm water.* This is essential for proper feather condition, especially in an indoor heated atmosphere, and should be done several times a week. Many owners will not bathe their birds in the winter, for fear they may catch cold, but this is in fact a critical time, since the heating is on in the house, and this will make the bird's plumage very dry. Most birds enjoy a shower, but some will actively dislike it. Nevertheless, the owner should persevere for the sake of the long-term plumage quality.

- *The provision of a stimulating and interesting environment.* This includes materials that can be chewed. There are many parrot toys available that are useful, but these can be expensive. It is just as effective to provide cheap replaceable objects such as clean twigs from non-toxic trees (fruit trees, willow, hazel, chestnut, eucalyptus), cardboard rolls or egg boxes, hide chews intended for dogs, or similar items. Birds need to gnaw, and these items may be destroyed and replaced cheaply on a regular basis, and may distract the bird from chewing its own feathers. Leaving a radio or television playing when the house is empty can be useful, but balance this with what I mentioned earlier about an over-busy environment. It may help to move the bird around to be with the family at different times of day, but conversely other birds fare much better if their housing is stable, and they can feel safe and secure. Each case has to be treated individually.

- *The provision of a well-balanced diet.* This is very important, and many cases of poor feather quality will be improved with better nutrition. Fussy eaters can be given one of the many vitamin and mineral supplements that are available, but of particular importance to feather growth are the amino acids to be found in animal protein. Many people seem surprised to be told that their pet birds should be given such items as hard cheese,

cooked egg or chicken, fish fingers and the like, but in fact the protein content of these foods is essential for new feather growth. Most wild parrots are facultative omnivores, which means they will eat anything that is available in their environment, including the occasional grub, caterpillar, insect, or even small fish, so animal protein is not at all alien to their diet. This subject is covered in more detail in Chapter 6.

Other remedies that may be adopted in specific cases could be the judicious use of hormone therapy, or the provision of a proper environment in which to pair off and breed.

Many other suggested methods really just attack the results of the plucking, and do not address the root cause. These would include the use of sedatives or psyche-altering drugs such as the much-publicized Prozac. These may have a place and a

Coco fitted with a conventional perspex 'Elizabethan' style collar. In dogs and cats this is generally coned forwards. In parrots it must be coned back over the shoulders to allow the bird to use its beak and feet to climb around. It is clear that the collar has been reinforced with parcel tape, yet still the bird has managed to nibble the edge. The owner has attached the wood and rope toy to distract and occupy the bird.

Perspex collar brace. This allows the parrot more freedom to access his food and water bowls, but theoretically keeps the neck too rigid to turn round to bite at its body feathers. In practice many persistent parrots are agile enough to get round it. The two halves of the collar are bolted together, and an Elizabethan collar may be screwed to it.

My current preference is to use a similarly shaped brace made from soft sponge pipe-lagging, wrapped around to hold it in place with cohesive bandage.

short-term effect in some cases, but usually once therapy is withdrawn, the plucking will recur if the bird's circumstances are unchanged. The beak may be notched or have a ball applied to its tip to prevent damage to the feathers; or collars may be attached to restrict plucking. Again, both these methods are preventive rather than curative, but may have a place in allowing feather recovery while

the underlying reasons are addressed. The fitting of collars is a personal preference: in my experience many birds are adept at removing them, or if they can't, then they become even more neurotic.

In summary, there is no overnight solution, and there is no single remedy suitable for all cases. Detailed 'psychoanalysis' is required for each bird (and very often its owner!), and even then there will be many disappointments. It will take weeks to correct a problem and establish new feather growth, but only a few minutes for a recalcitrant bird to pull them all out again. Many cases do relapse, and with repeated plucking there may well be permanent follicular damage that means the bird will never grow feathers in these areas.

Parrots are intelligent creatures, and require both mental and physical stimulation to keep them fit. This they have in their natural wild environment, so I repeat that feather plucking is a disease of captivity. Each case presents a challenge to owner and veterinarian, and every attempt must be made to solve the underlying problem rather than merely to suppress the urge to pluck. Many of the remedies for behavioural feather-plucking will be addressed in the following chapter, along with other varieties of troublesome behaviour.

CHAPTER 10

Behaviour and Training

Parrots are intelligent, inquisitive, demanding, long-lived birds. At the same time – with the exception of budgerigars, cockatiels, and perhaps lovebirds – *they are not domesticated species*. They are just a few generations removed from their wild ancestors. They therefore retain many of the instinctive behaviour patterns of their wild cousins, associated with survival, foraging, and communication over long distances.

Yet we have bred them in captivity and hand-reared them within human families. We expect them to fit into our lifestyles and our behaviour patterns. We want them to be as biddable as the pet dog, and as permanently cuddly as the docile, loving babies they were when we collected them at twelve weeks old from the pet store. They are sociable birds, yet we expect them to live for decades in isolation in a wire prison, with eventually just perfunctory attention to food and water, as the novelty of the 'new toy' or 'status symbol' wears off. We find we cannot cope with the mess, the destructiveness, and the screaming.

Is it any wonder then that so many of these beautiful birds end up being passed from home to home, and ending up in parrot sanctuaries or rescue centres? It is not their fault: it is entirely the result of our ignorance and misunderstanding of parrots' nutritional, physical, and emotional needs, and our misinterpretation of the signals they give out. It is often the case that mixing with others of their own kind will resolve their psychological confusion, but sadly so many of these poor

birds are permanently damaged by our inability to provide properly for them.

Sanctuaries themselves are founded by good-hearted people who want to do the best for these damaged, unwanted parrots, but they quickly become inundated with people's cast-offs. This increases pressure on the sanctuary – lack of space, time, and money will mean that rescued individuals can end up in worse conditions than they were before. The best that can be said is that

A Green-winged macaw (Ara chloroptera) at a parrot show. This bird, according to its owner, 'lived outside in the fresh air'. Yes – in this cage, hence its decrepit rusty condition!

at least they are with others of their own kind. Obviously there are some very good, well-funded and managed parrot rescue centres, but there are too few out there.

Taking into account all of the above, it is clear that there is too little education for the pet-owning public and the pet-bird trade on the welfare needs of parrots. As shown in the subjects covered in this book there is a general dearth of knowledge, especially where it applies to the contentment and appropriate behaviour of pet birds.

CAPTIVE LIFESTYLE

Wild parrots are raised by their parents in a dark nest, fed small frequent meals, and grow quickly to full size. However, their mental and emotional development continues after fledging and is dependent upon spending some time with their parents as well as other young birds, learning how to be a bird. Avian social skills like flying, foraging, feeding, and a social hierarchy within the group are paramount. Mutual grooming occurs between parent and offspring, and bonded adult pairs, but rarely with other members of the flock. Gradually, usually after several years, these young individuals will reach sexual maturity, pair off, and breed for themselves.

In the captive pet situation, we bring a very young baby, that has possibly been reared in isolation with exclusively human contact, into a bewildering human home environment. We shower it with affection, stroking and cuddling it incessantly, and pandering to its every whim. We allow it to dominate our lives, perching on head or shoulders, and treat it at least as an equal, if not the 'star of the show'. The young parrot will have no opportunity to learn how to be a bird; neither is it taught any form of 'pecking order'. Instead of interacting with a parent or older cousins, it is allowed rapidly to become the 'flock leader' in the household.

The youngster is subjected by its human handlers to 'grooming' that is inadvertently sexually stimulating – stroking over the rump and tail base. This will encourage early adolescence, and inappropriate 'pair bonding' with a member of the household. This may progress to jealousy and aggression towards other members of the family. As the bird matures, sexual frustration will increase as it does not receive the natural responses its instincts suggest should be forthcoming. We need to approach our pet parrots much more along the lines of a 'parent-child' relationship.

THE BIGGEST PROBLEMS

Perhaps the three most common behavioural patterns that cause parrot-keepers considerable distress and difficulty are feather-plucking, screaming and biting.

Owner investigating the tail base of her Umbrella cockatoo. Note the new pink blood feathers growing in the tail, and the brush-tip of the preen gland. However, touching this area is sexually stimulating to the bird, and will lead to frustration.

Feather-Plucking

As explained in the preceding chapter, feather-plucking is a very complex condition, with a wide variety of possible causes. These causes need to be investigated thoroughly before making a diagnosis of 'behavioural' or 'psychological' feather-plucking.

Screaming

Vocalization is perfectly normal behaviour in these highly social birds, and it is quite normal for parrots to have noisy periods at dawn and dusk. This is when they would naturally be waking from their roost, communicating with others in the flock, then setting off to forage for food. At the end of the day they return to their resting places, keeping in contact with each other before settling for the night. In the breeding season they will vocalize to attract a mate and to warn off rival suitors.

Many of these birds come from areas of dense vegetation, and they use their calls to locate each other when they cannot be seen. It is therefore quite normal for your parrot to call out to you to keep in contact when you leave the room and he does not know where you have gone. The problem is that many of these birds have naturally very loud voices to penetrate the thick vegetation, to cover long distances, and to be heard above the calls of other creatures.

If you don't like the noise, then don't keep a parrot! The problem generally arises when the noise becomes unacceptable to neighbours, or to members of the household who are not so fond of parrots.

Adult Green-winged macaw. That huge beak is a formidable weapon and can inflict a painful bite. It is not surprising that many people feel scared when around these birds, yet if approached with understanding and confidence they can be very gentle.

Biting

Sexual Behaviour

Aggressive behaviour is most commonly the result of our failure to read the parrot's body language and to pick up the warning signs. Individual birds may well be territorially aggressive in the breeding season (notably Amazons and some macaws) and will protect their cage, a favourite toy, a companion bird, or even their perceived 'mate' in the human household against invasion by other members of the family.

Hand-reared parrots, especially when raised in 'solitary confinement' away from other parrots, will have no fear of humans but at the same time will have confusions of identity when they reach sexual maturity. These birds will attempt to mate with their owners, while fiercely repelling 'advances' from other members of the family.

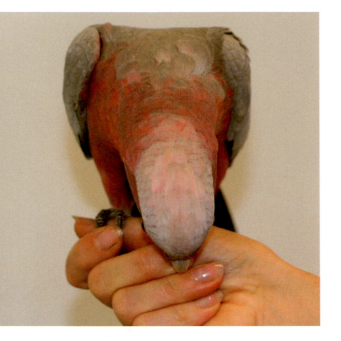

Young Galah cockatoo 'testing' its perch of soft human flesh. This is natural inquisitive behaviour. (Note the duller colouration compared with that of adult birds elsewhere in this book.)

Beak as a Tool

Most cases of biting occur because we misunderstand the parrot's intentions. Very often the bird is simply reaching out, using its beak as a tool to climb up or to test its environment. The confident owner will allow the parrot to support its body weight momentarily while it takes a step up with its feet. This is the way that parrots get around in trees and bushes, or their cages.

The diffident owner though, being wary of that huge powerful beak, will tremble or withdraw the finger just as the parrot goes to hold on. The bird's instinctive reaction to this unstable, wobbly perch is inevitably to hold on tighter, but because the 'perch' is soft flesh, the result to the human is painful! The owner needs to remain confident and hold the hand steady and firm if the bird is not to become unstable and hold on tightly. (Conversely, a bird that is misbehaving on the hand may be distracted by a sudden jerk of the hand – the 'earthquake' technique.)

Hello Stranger!

Alternatively, the human gets bitten because they do not realize that this is the parrot's last line of defence against perceived attack. *Parrots are prey species*: they do not normally attack and eat other animals. Their eyes are therefore sited on the side of their heads, to give good wide-angle vision to detect approaching danger. *Humans on the other hand are predators*, with binocular forward-facing eyes. A cat or dog will happily approach a human face-to-face and lick them on the nose, as they are also predators, but a parrot would find this intimidating.

A familiar owner will be accepted, but a stranger advancing on a parrot and saying 'who's a pretty boy then' will be perceived by the terrified bird as a potential killer. The bird will do all it can to ward off the attack – raising its head feathers, lifting its wings and squawking, fanning its tail and flashing its eyes – and as a last resort will retreat by flying away. If the bird cannot fly away because it is cornered, and if the 'aggressor' continues its advance, then the parrot will defend itself in the only way left to it, by biting its attacker. This is not the bird's fault – it is the result of the ignorant human not realizing how scary they appear to the bird.

MANAGEMENT AND TRAINING

Avoidance of major behaviour problems depends on an early understanding of the parrot's emotional and physical needs, and the correct 'parent-child' approach.

It is useful for a parrot to learn a few simple commands and instructions, and to have 'life-style parameters' that will give guidance as to what is acceptable behaviour in its home environment. Parrots are quick to learn, and will soon accept routine feeding times, rest periods, owners' working hours, as well as 'step up', 'no' and other simple commands.

However, many parrots will already have developed problem behaviours, and trying to modify these can be difficult. There will be many suggestions, like 'get him a mate', 'smack him on the beak', 'squirt him with water', most of which are less than helpful. Animal behaviourists will talk about 'positive and negative reinforcement', 'antecedents', 'possessive aggression' and the like.

Reward and Encouragement

Basically what it boils down to is rewarding and encouraging the required behaviour, and ignoring (or at least not reinforcing) the unwanted behaviour.

Behaviour modification will require time, commitment, and patience on the part of the handler. 'Training' sessions should be brief but frequent: parrots will tire quickly after a few minutes. Understanding the bird's body language and signs of fear, annoyance, threat, or other emotion is paramount. Respect the bird's quiet periods when it wants to rest, and do not try to have a training session then.

Yelling and shouting will get you nowhere. This will be entertaining and stimulating to the bird, and will sound like its natural vocalizing. Thus running to your parrot shouting 'No!' or 'Stop it!' when he pulls out a feather or has a screaming fit will simply make him do it all the more because he enjoys the game.

Try distraction – not by offering a titbit, because that is also rewarding the bad behaviour – but by pretending to do something that the parrot may find interesting. Play with his toys or hang new toys somewhere else in the room, out of his immediate reach. Sing or dance. Let your bird know where you are: individuals of the flock stay in touch by calling to each other, and a single pet bird may panic if he cannot see you. Call out or whistle reassuringly from another room, but do not rush back in when he calls out, otherwise he will keep on doing it.

Talk in a whisper. Your bird will quieten down and try to listen to what you are saying. When he responds in dulcet tones rather than screaming, continue to talk quietly and offer a treat.

Rewards may be food – give those beloved sunflower seeds as treats only, and not as the major part of his food bowl, or use peanuts in shell, grapes, or pistachios – whatever is your bird's absolute favourite. Or you could simply approach and talk to your bird, giving the attention he craves. Tickle his head – parrots cannot easily groom their own head feathers, and love to be preened in this area by their companions.

Blue and yellow macaw having his head tickled. Most parrots enjoy this form of contact, which mimics that of mutual grooming from a mate or parent.

Blue-fronted Amazon enjoying contact with its owner in another way, by holding 'hands'.

Timing is critical – the reward or response should immediately follow the action, so that the two events are connected by the parrot. It certainly is entirely counter-productive to scream and scold your bird when he is sitting quietly on top of his cage, having destroyed the arm of your chair while you were out of the room two hours ago. He will simply think that you are a crazy human, or that you want to have a shouting game!

'DOMINANCE'

The idea is not to seek to 'dominate' or control the bird. We seek rather to understand and channel normal behaviour patterns.

It is frequently quoted that parrots in a dominant position – that is, above your eye level – will be difficult to manage. To an extent this is true: the bird feels safe when he is high up out of reach of danger. It is more about confidence and safety than dominance. Conversely, if he is on the floor, he will be more inclined to step up onto your hand or a stick so that he can escape from the dangerous place low down. Either way, you will have more success if you keep your parrot in front of you and below your eye level.

Work with your bird in a quiet area, with subdued lighting, so that the parrot is relaxed when being trained. Do not attempt it when he is either excited and worked up, or grumpy and tired. Each bird is an individual – do not expect yours to behave in the same way that your friend's does.

These are very general guidelines, and severe behavioural problems will generally require the assistance of an experienced avian behaviourist. However, I hope I have given you food for thought and some basic ideas to enable you to include a parrot in your life as a safe, calm, enjoyable family pet.

Black-headed Caique perched comfortably on his owner's forearm. He is visible to the owner and below eye level.

Amazon parrot and a young child in perfect harmony, completely at ease with each other.
(Photo: Jan Hooimeijer)

CHAPTER 11

What of the Future?

Parrot keeping has changed dramatically in the thirty years that I have been involved with it, and it will continue to do so. There are fewer hobbyist breeders of the larger species, but many more pet birds. There has thankfully been a big reduction in the trade in wild-caught parrots, but we still have a long way to go.

In many places in the world, parrots' natural habitat is still disappearing at an alarming rate. Increased environmental awareness and dissatisfaction with global greed will hopefully lead to a progressive reduction in pressure on the dwindling wild places of the world, much of which is home to these spectacular creatures.

Conservation groups have had great success in setting up local reserves and rehabilitating some endangered species, as well as informing the indigenous people of the value to them of protecting these birds for eco-tourism rather than catching and robbing their nests to sell the chicks for pennies. Local measures like the wrapping of tree trunks in metal (tinning) to prevent reptile predators climbing to parrot nests, and the planting of specific foodstuffs will continue to aid the survival of locally endangered species. Clearing nesting areas (especially small islands) of parrot predators will also protect breeding populations.

In other parts of the world, cockatoos and parakeets continue to flock in pest numbers, devastating agricultural business. Control measures are necessary in these situations, and will undoubtedly continue under licence. The successful and rapid spread of feral populations of non-indigenous species like the Ring-necked parakeet *(Psittacula krameri)* and the Quaker parakeet *(Myiopsitta monachus)* will inevitably lead to calls for their culling in some areas.

Advances in veterinary medicine across the board continue to be amazing, and owners are more aware of what vets can do. There are increasing numbers of graduates taking an interest in avian medicine and surgery, so hopefully more parrots will be better treated. We will learn more about the long-term infectious diseases like PBFD, PDD and psittacosis, and how better to control them.

Diets for parrots will continue to improve, with more and better-formulated products. The result will be better nourished and healthier parrots. There is increasing awareness of the emotional needs of these fascinating birds, and better understanding of their natural behaviour. This will lead to far better management of their lives in captivity, and hopefully a big reduction in the numbers of birds that end up in rescue centres as their owners give up on them.

It is quite likely that registration may be required to keep parrots, in the same way that pigeon and raptor keepers have to close-ring and register their birds. This will further improve and regulate the hobby, and should also ensure improvements in parrot welfare.

With regard to breeding birds, there will be reduced focus on double or treble-clutching to obtain more eggs, and less hand-rearing, with more parent-reared (and therefore better adjusted) young parrots. Artificial insemination will undoubtedly be used in rare or valuable individuals, as it already is in budgerigar breeding and birds of prey. The breeders of mutation varieties will continue their path to produce unusual colour and feather varieties of their chosen species, but other groups will strive to keep the nominate original species pure.

Or is this all a pipe dream? No matter what, it is certain that these attractive, colourful, lively birds will continue to play a big part in people's lives for generations to come, and I hope that I have managed to convey in this book something about understanding their needs and the best way to care for them so that they may have long and rewarding lives.

This book is dedicated to Eric and all others like him. These birds have enriched my life.

Acknowledgements

I would like to express my profound thanks to many people.

To my clients and their patients over the years who have entrusted me with their birds and taught me much – many of their birds have been pictured here. My friends and professional colleagues in the bird-keeping world, the Parrot Society, and the Association of Avian Veterinarians. In particular Tony Pittman, Nigel Harcourt-Brown, Steve Brookes, and Jan Hooimeijer, who have allowed me to use their photographs in this work.

To my grandfather Frederick, who taught me about garden birds and got me started. To my parents Ken and Mary who enabled me to have the education and support I needed to get this far. To my son and daughter Barnaby and Tiffany, and grandchildren Tilly and Jacob. You make me very proud.

To my nurse/receptionist/personal assistant Gail Masters, a loyal and supportive colleague, whose menagerie has supplied many of the photographs for this book. To Maria (and Dougal!) who has given unstinting support, patience and love in the hours that have been consumed in putting this altogether.

This is my legacy of thirty years of enjoyable and fascinating work with birds, and I hope it brings pleasure and help to a few more people. This work has been written from a distillation of my own thoughts and experience gained in over thirty years working with birds and bird keepers, witnessing a range of species, husbandry methods, housing and diets.

Further Information

I have consulted various texts and the internet to check my facts when necessary – mostly the spelling of scientific names of parrots – but none of this work uses quoted references. These days a list of recommended further reading or useful contacts becomes out of date almost before the book is published, and with worldwide book sales a society or rescue centre based in the UK would be useless to a reader in Australia. Most researchers now in any case use internet search engines for their information.

However, I will suggest the following organizations, all with informative websites, giving current and relevant contact details, with links to related groups.

The Association of Avian Veterinarians
www.aav.org

The Parrot Society UK
www.theparrotsocietyuk.org
The World Parrot Trust
www.parrots.org

Local areas will have their pet insurers, alarm installers, local boarding facilities, clubs and societies, wire manufacturers and toy makers, all of which may be found on-line.

Readers may also find of interest the following websites of some of the people who generously contributed photographs of parrots to this book:

www.bluemacaws.org (Tony Pittman)
www.stichtingpapegaai.nl (Jan Hooimeijer DVM)
www.wildparrotsupclose.co.uk (Steve Brookes)

Index